Time's Unfading Garden

Anne Spencer (about 1940)

Time's Unfading Garden

Anne Spencer's Life

and Poetry 🌿 🌿 🌿

J. LEE GREENE

Louisiana State University Press
Baton Rouge and London

Copyright © 1977 by Louisiana State University Press
All rights reserved
Manufactured in the United States of America
Designer: Albert Crochet
Type face: VIP Palatino
Typesetter: Graphic World, Inc., St. Louis, Missouri
Printer and binder: Kingsport Press, Kingsport, Tennessee

LIBRARY OF CONGRESS CATALOGING IN PUBLICATION DATA

Greene, J   Lee, 1944–
    Time's unfading garden.

    Bibliography: p.
    Includes index.
        1.   Spencer, Anne, 1882–1975.   2.   Poets, American—
20th century—Biography.   I.   Spencer, Anne, 1882–1975.
II.   Title.
PS3537.P444Z65   811'.5'2   77–5960
ISBN 0–8071–0294–6

Contents

Illustrations

Acknowledgments

I am indebted to several people and institutions for assistance in the completion of this study. I wish especially to extend my gratitude to Bethel Spencer Stevenson, Alroy Spencer Rivers, Chauncey E. Spencer, and Anne (Mrs. Chauncey E.) Spencer for their help in the collection and use of material for this study. Grace Nail (Mrs. James Weldon) Johnson and Yale University Library gave their permission for me to quote from letters between James Weldon Johnson and Anne Spencer contained in the James Weldon Johnson Memorial Collection of Negro Arts and Letters, Collection of American Literature, Beinecke Rare Book and Manuscript Library. Yale University Library also granted me permission to quote from letters between Anne Spencer and Carl Van Vechten and Harold Jackman contained in the Carl Van Vechten Collection, Collection of American Literature, Beinecke Rare Book and Manuscript Library. The National Endowment for the Humanities provided a research grant which allowed me to complete the initial phase of this study. And Anne Spencer and Chauncey E. Spencer allowed me to print poems by Anne Spencer and to quote from materials in the Spencer Family Papers in the Anne Spencer House and Garden Historic Landmark, Lynchburg, Virginia.

Time's Unfading Garden

1 ✂ Early Life

It is not difficult to see similarities between Anne Spencer's life and writings and those of some nineteenth-century American writers: the transcendental musings of Ralph Waldo Emerson, the independence and nonconformity of Henry David Thoreau, or the habit of composing cryptic poems on bits and pieces of paper as did Emily Dickinson. This does not mean that in chronology or merit she stands with these three in American literary history, but perhaps as a poet she has more in common with nineteenth-century American writers than she does either with twentieth-century American poets or with the general development of black American literature which culminated in the movement often termed the Harlem Renaissance, the period to which she historically belongs as a poet. A study of her life and writings can stand on its own, independent of the degree to which she is like or unlike other American writers, past or present. The poetry itself is intrinsically worth study, and attention to her life is exacted by the achievement of her poetry.

Anne Spencer was forty years old when her first poem was published. Reading her small canon of poetry today, one might not readily ascertain the personality behind the poems. Many of her poetic themes are the themes of her life, especially the emphasis on freedom and love. If her poetry was unconventional for a black writer during the time in which it was published, so was her entire life characterized by unconventionality. Though the themes of her poetry and life are closely aligned, the content of each is quite different. She was a "controversial" figure all her life, yet her poetry for the most part cannot be termed controversial. Few of her poems express or capture the intensity of her adult life and life-style during the seventy-five years she lived in a town which she considered victimized by racial bigotry and social friction. From the poems one would probably never guess the incidents which marked the life of Anne Spencer in her constant struggle to rise above social and racial restrictions. Her poetry exhibits an aesthetic control which elevates it above mere polemics. The freedom expressed in her poems is human freedom, not ethnic propaganda; the love of which she writes is human love, love not bound by racial differences; the psychology and aspirations of the generation she depicts are not limited to particular times, places, or peoples.

The woman and her writings go hand in hand: to understand the person better, one needs to look at her poetry; to understand the poetry, it is helpful to review her life. Her best poetry can stand alone; the formalist critic can find it as rewarding as the biographical critic. But knowledge of the poet's life makes the poetry even more challenging and interesting.

I once asked Mrs. Spencer why she never had written a novel. Her reply: "I've been too busy living one." Many years earlier she made practically the same statement in a sketch of her life which she wrote for her children, later qualifying it by adding: "This is a silly, egotistic thing to say."[1] Yet it is that egotistic humanitarianism which suggests Thoreau's similar statement: "My life has been the poem I would have writ,/But I could not both live and utter it." Preparatory to a discussion of her beginnings as a published poet and to an examination of her writings, a sketch of the life of the woman will illuminate the career of the poet.

Mrs. Spencer remembered little about her life with her mother and father as a family unit on the plantation where she was born in Henry County, Virginia, February 6, 1882. But she remembered well her heartbreak and confusion when the family sepa-

---

1. This autobiographical sketch, dated November, 1959, is now part of the Spencer Family Papers at the Anne Spencer House and Garden Historic Landmark, Lynchburg, Virginia.

rated, though she was fifteen years old before she learned from her mother the events that led to the separation. Both her parents were proud and strong-willed people, each in a different way. In essence, her mother's emphasis on manners and morals and her father's emphasis on security and manhood produced a clash of personalities which led to the eventual separation. Her parents were members of the first generation of the freed race to reach adulthood. Because there was a family history which she did not wish to publicize, Mrs. Spencer requested that surnames not be used for her parents. Of her parents Mrs. Spencer once wrote: "Fate let them escape chattel slavery by a hair. Good thing, too, for the slaveowner!" [2] The ancestry of her father, Joel Cephus, is traced primarily to the Seminole Indians. In the early 1840s the last of the Seminole Indians were removed from Florida to territories beyond the Mississippi River. Joel's forebears supposedly did not move with the other Seminoles, but migrated northward and settled for a while near Raleigh, North Carolina. Later they migrated into southern Virginia where Joel was born. A descendant of mixed black, white, and Indian ancestry, Joel Cephus, according to Mrs. Spencer, was born a slave in Henry County, Virginia, in 1862. As a young adult, his pride was a driving force as he struggled to shake off the "scent of slavery" and to establish economic security and a positive sense of his own manhood. His sense of self made him disdain working for others, and his pride made him scorn having to answer to anyone.

In her Notebooks [3] Anne Spencer briefly characterizes her mother's origins: "Mother's memory, as long as she drew natural breath, was excellent. Yet she could forget, as when she de-

2. *Ibid.*
3. Some of the material for this study is taken from notes Mrs. Spencer wrote about her life and writings expressly for me. She also made available for my use materials which she had written over at least a fifty-year period. Excepting a very few items, all of this material is without dates, page numbers, or any readily identifiable method of organization. For convenience, then, I will refer to all of her written materials as comprising her Notebooks, though the materials are not contained in nor were they designed for a formal notebook. The Notebooks are now part of the Spencer Family Papers.

clared that she was born free and *ekal*. Slips like that were rare, even when she was trying to forget by insisting —for certainly she had to take her 'story,' as I am giving my own now, by hearsay. Her refusal was stoutly reiterated: I was born free and *ekal* —tho once, I remember her adding, it left its scent on us, all of us. I smell yet!" Sarah Louise, the poet's mother, was born in 1866 in Patrick County, Virginia. She was an illegitimate child; her mother was a former slave and her father a wealthy Virginia aristocrat. Sarah never used her father's name, a name, Mrs. Spencer pointed out, well known in American aristocracy of the nineteenth and twentieth centuries. Apparently her mother's name was Scales, for Sarah used this as her own maiden name. Though she probably never courted recognition by her father or his family, and received neither social nor economic notice from either, she was proud of her ancestry and maintained an aristocratic attitude throughout her life—an attitude which often manifested itself in a condescension toward others whom she felt socially beneath her. But she was a "working aristocrat," fighting, as was Joel, to establish a life of social and economic respectability, but concerned strongly with manners and morals.

The two lived on nearby plantations in southwestern Virginia —Joel in Henry County and Sarah in Patrick County—before they married. And on the plantation where they took up residence, Sarah, at age sixteen, gave birth to the couple's only child, Annie Bethel. The earliest memory Mrs. Spencer could recall of her life was a visit to her birthplace:

There has been almost a century of this [thing] called living, or is it two in one—an experience so closely tight that that could have happened. The first memory: They said I was maybe three; 2 cabins on an easy slanting hill, fenced with rails, nutting weather. I was (and blacks and whites, alphabetically, think that rape is a 10-commandment word) being walked, pushed and carried by a group of not too solicitous older children. That was when my brain took the picture that has never left me: A man with a gun came around the curved road, calling out in fright, "get up the hill, get over the fence, we are trying to track a mad dog—get up the hill!" I remember my hands. They were clutching the [walnut] shells that would not let go, as I was lifted clumsily up and over.

All one's days, the moves made—the scrambles—seem just that foolish. Here was a man, a gun; "over the fence" was total unprotection; a whole field between us and the roadway. No one. The place seemed uninhabited, except for ourselves. Yet they told me that was my home where I was born. Since then that senseless stumbling forward into all these years.

[Notebooks]

Joel Cephus was a very stern, grave man. As he saw it, his duty lay in providing for his young family and securing that economic independence for which he yearned. He found it distasteful and personally degrading to have to answer to a "boss" or to have to take orders from those who would employ him. Whatever Joel Cephus was doing to make a living in rural Henry County before and shortly after his marriage, he was disgusted with it. He thought that a move closer to a town and a new job in which he could be his own boss would allow him much of that personal and economic freedom which he desired. About 1883 he moved with his wife and baby to Martinsville, Virginia, a town near Danville: "Joel had saved some money, somehow. They came into Martinsville, I was about a year old. Mother said 'they were cutting stone and building the Richmond & Danville railroad. Your father, who swore he would never work for anybody again, opened a saloon in Martinsville'" (Notebooks).

For quite some time he ran the "rough bar" in Martinsville, a bar whose customers were mostly Italians and other white minorities in the area. Joel did not make a lot of money from his business. But scorning any necessity of blacks having to work for whites, "he would not let Sarah hire out to make money. On occasions he would give her small amounts of money for her own use." [4] Sarah seldom spent the money she was able to acquire from the rare and covert occasions when she found employment; she saved her earnings and the "dimes and quarters" Joel gave her for her personal use, with the intent of using her

4. All quotations from Mrs. Spencer in this study not specifically attributed to the Notebooks come from a series of interviews and telephone conversations I had with her between March, 1971, and June, 1975.

savings for a plan which she conceived a few years after their marriage.

Sarah was a religious woman and occasionally she and Annie attended a Methodist church in the area. Apparently Joel was not very religious. He was a "go-getter" and was primarily concerned with saving his money. "My father would take me and my two dolls (I still have one of them) over to this saloon and I would show how intelligent I was." The men in the saloon were amused with Annie's "showing-off" and "would throw big copper pennies" at her. A precocious as well as an extremely beautiful child, Annie, at Joel's urgings, would parade up and down the bar of the saloon and entertain the customers with her wit, intelligence, and beauty when she was between one and a half and four years old. This whole practice of showing off Annie at the bar, especially for profit, "just kept up a noise and argument" between Joel and Sarah. "Mother never wanted me to be raised around white men," and her "inherited pride" would not let her submit to such humiliation. "Mother made up her mind that she couldn't allow this thing to go on."

My parents, like many unlike coupled people, used me in a doting way as their warm war coldly pursued [on] their personal battleground. He would have, in even a now condition of semicitizenhood, made superior engines of commerce on war, for like Dickens' Gradgrind he believed facts—demonstrable facts—and any other category of life he was ready to track down for the kill. Still, for the about six years they were together, my father was memorable to me.

House, not home, but an abatis holding both the attacked and the attacker within the fork. These two have been a sign and a textbook for me all of my perplexed thinking life, even deep in childhood up and apart as now, to be studied, felt, seen, tasted with my mind; the stink of slavery still on them. They were Sarah Louise and Joel Cephus. No one called him Joe. He was literate. Somehow had taught himself "to read, write and 'figger' better than any white man in Martinsville, and never intended to be hired to a damn one 'em again." That was the letter he wrote me in 1893—on his way to the Chicago World's Fair. [It probably was Sarah rather than Joel who went to the fair that year.] "My name Joel is from the Bible; call me by it." And Mother said they did.

[Notebooks]

Mrs. Spencer said that her recollections about the "warm war coldly pursued" between her parents were more of the general atmosphere surrounding the situation and her own psychological trauma as a result than of the details of the problems between her parents, which culminated in the "tragedy on the barroom floor" and precipitated the family's break as a unit. From what she could recall of the saloon, "There was not a Negro in the whole place, just Greeks and Italians, and so on. One day Mother came in and said, 'I came to get my daughter.' She reached for me and my father jerked me away from her. Mother said, 'He grabbed me [Sarah] and turned up my clothes and spanked me. A few men were in the place at the time. Do you know, Annie, I was clean but I didn't even have on my hamburg [bloomer]!'" Sarah told Annie of this embarrassing incident when Annie was fifteen, and when Sarah thought she would be able to understand the whole situation. "I understood Mother a little better after she told me that." Noting that Joel's "prostitution" of Annie had been going on since Annie was less than two years old, Sarah recounted, as Mrs. Spencer later recorded, the "tragedy on the barroom floor":

[We moved to Martinsville and Joel opened a saloon, Sarah said.] "I was a little over 17 then. He would not allow me to work nor even come into the place. Joel bought whatever we actually needed . . . [and seldom let me handle or make money].

[He had been taking you over to the saloon for quite some time.] "But this time, I promised myself, was the end! He had you over there all afternoon. It was growing dark. You were then a little over four. I slipped over, went in. The usual crowd. He was the only Negro in the place. He grinned and frowned at the same time. 'What you want?' As usual you were up on the bar counter. 'I want my daughter,' as I took your hand. Don't you remember?" she asked me. I shook my head.

"Then Joel—I was skinny then—jerked my hand and never sitting down bent one knee, turned my skirts and spanked my behind. You were crying. The men were quiet."

Then my mother gave me one of her somehow pitiable, quaint, slanted looks, in the same [way] she still used when after the chore of learning to sign her name she'd say, "It may be right, but it looks funny!" This time—continuing her confidence, preparing her daughter for life's long track—this time she added, "and I didn't have my [deep] hamburg drawers on!" So long ago, then. And now my own trousseau had seven pairs with six-inch hamburg, ruffled, starched leg—scratching things—and a leghorn and a pink peau de soie. That furnished the only geography of the [world] I knew or cared about.

My memory and the time and place fix what it was—a rowdy drinking place; no women, no black denizen, but a sort of murky everybody —so much so that I cannot recall my father looking any different than the other men. . . .

My mother shed tears. "How could they let a child do a thing like that?" Looking back I say how could you beget such a quick-hearted child—for it's a lifelong affliction. No sensible, organized, deliberate thing is in *doing my own thing*. [Here is?] my definite sin: to want back—even every thought and irregular act in a century of living—to annihilate!

[Notebooks]

As an adolescent and as an adult, Mrs. Spencer tried to recall her life with her parents and the barroom incident. But her image never was in sharp focus. She always could remember "a child's hands sticky with a candy stick," her metaphor for the joys of that period, interrupted by the turbulence within the family. "A change did come. . . . And a child remembers and shudders for years. No physical thing needed, but still the anger in voices and hard eyes and mouths speaking. The mouth saying, but eyes are worse. How was a child to know that this was too a savage state and existed . . . all over the slums and in palaces over the earth. . . . What could a child know then or now? Release came" (Notebooks).

After this humiliating "barroom scene" Sarah made up her mind to leave Joel and take Annie with her: "My father was saving of what his trade in drink brought, but he had a weakness for 'fine clothes'—for me, himself and Mother—which he bought to his taste. Mother liked—overliked—to be well-dressed also. This determination to get away and lack of money kept her hemletting for over a year after her mind was clear about what must be done" (Notebooks). Sarah wrote (or had someone to write for her) to either her brother George in Pineville, Kentucky, or Nathan in Bramwell, West Virginia, about her plans and he sent her some money, "barely enough for one fare—not a half fare for me" (Notebooks), to leave Martinsville. For about two years after the spanking incident she hoarded dimes and quarters from the money Joel gave her and from her own earnings until she had enough, with what her brother sent, to leave Martinsville—but not enough to support herself and Annie for any length of time. Her first impulse was to go to West Virginia where Nathan lived with his family in the mining district. But she soon abandoned the idea of taking Annie immediately to West Virginia: she did not want to burden her relatives with the possibility of having to support two more people; the uncertainties of being able to support herself and her child adequately were too overwhelming; and, moreover, she would not subject Annie to the living conditions of families in the coal mining communities.

"My mother had a friend, Mrs. Clark, in Winston-Salem, North Carolina. When she first left my father, she took me to her friend in Winston-Salem and I stayed there that winter." This separation from both her parents is what in her Notebooks Mrs. Spencer termed her "first firmly realized tragedy." It probably was in the fall of 1887 or 1888 when Sarah left Annie in Winston-Salem and then went alone to Bramwell, West Virginia, where her brother Nathan lived. Sarah was determined but not certain that she could make it on her own, or that she would eventually find work to support herself and her small child. One problem had been solved temporarily, however; Sarah was sure Annie had been comfortably placed.

After Sarah and Annie had left, Joel, for a short time at least, remained in the Martinsville area but later, according to Mrs. Spencer's son, moved to Stony Island or Pullman, Illinois, where he worked for the Stony Island Railroad Company. Eventually he moved to San Bernadino, California, and established a prosperous business there.

Once in West Virginia Sarah secured a job as a "cook boss" in the Blue Stone Inn in Bramwell. During the winter she was able to save some money for the life she saw ahead. "When Mother found out that she was going to do well [on her own], she sent money." Sarah also sent instructions. "She said that I must go to Sunday school and take music. I think I went to something like a kindergarten for a while. The lady who lived behind us taught me music on a small organ for twenty-five cents per lesson. Nobody could ever teach me music or to sing; they gave up on me at the Seminary."

Though the Clark family did enter me in primer grade school, there's nothing remembered except a little boy whose face I smacked when he came marching and someone yelled "she's his sweetheart." My vocabulary was minus that word. We became friends because I wanted to use him: Near where the Clarks lived, on a back street there was a place to eat and sleep (another I did not know). I found that sweetheart at six could read, write and tell time—each skill involved in *my* larger experience here—and I could do neither, though I was such a bright, clever child, the kind that in age fools any teacher . . . and I wanted a name put over the sand piles I'd patted up—Ants' Hotel.

That year though was good for me. It poled a feeling for the actual earth itself that I had inborn, suffused and enlightened, without which nothing that one is born in has lift or meaning, but somehow and somewhere one must make contact, touch earth, and be willing to share earth with the other [combatants?].

I was so mad at that kid in the Learning Tree. Shucks, I ran on *ants' hotel* 82 years before I would concede the Learning Tree, because the earth itself is made for learning as Heaven for knowing.

[Notebooks]

That Christmas Sarah visited Annie in Winston-Salem. This was probably the only time she visited her before she came the following Easter to pick her up and take her to Bramwell to live. Annie was still too young then to understand what was happening to her life and to her family.

From what Mrs. Spencer and Mrs. Edward Palmer (Annie's childhood friend Lucille Dixie) could recall, Bramwell, West Virginia, was a beautiful small town in the 1880s. "In Bramwell the Blue Stone River encompassed the town in the form of a horseshoe. It had a population of about two hundred and fifty when I lived there—must have one hundred and seventy-five now," Mrs. Spencer said, laughing. Mrs. Palmer recalled that there was a hotel, the Blue Stone Inn where Sarah worked, at least one grocery store, a small post office, a very fashionable seamstress shop, a school, two churches, and some stylish houses. Like many of the small towns in the area, Bramwell was named after one of the prominent men connected with the operation or ownership of the coal mines. The fashionable little town "boasted about nine millionaires" and was reserved for the mine operators and probably some of the owners. It was not a town for miners. The miners—many of Polish and Hungarian descent, Negroes, and others who had come to the area to work the coal mines (at least seventeen different ethnic groups [5])—lived outside the town.

About one-half mile out of town there were the Negro Blue Stone Baptist Church and the Negro school, Mrs. Palmer recalled. The school was for the sons and daughters of the blacks who worked in the mines and those who worked in the town as domestics or in service positions; it was not patronized by the small and exclusive "black bourgeoisie" of Bramwell. It was a two-room frame school which accommodated six grades.

For a short while after arriving in Bramwell, Annie stayed with her "aunts and uncles down at the mines." But, fearing that she could not work and adequately care for Annie at the same time, Sarah sought to place her in one of the "best black homes" in the town. Her alternatives for a foster home were limited since there were few black families in Bramwell, and even fewer who met Sarah's standards. In fact, as far as Sarah was concerned, the "black bourgeoisie" of Bramwell was composed of three families: the minister's, the doctor's, and the barber's. She soon eliminated the minister's family as a possible choice. Dr. W. A. Holley, who was brought to Bramwell by the mine owners as a physician for the blacks who worked in the mines, had perhaps the economically "best" black household in

5. For information on the coal mining industry in southwestern West Virginia and the ethnic groups involved, see Jerry Bruce Thomas, "Coal Country: The Rise of the Southern Smokeless Coal Industry and Its Effect on Area Development, 1872–1910" (Ph.D. dissertation, University of North Carolina at Chapel Hill, 1971).

Bramwell. Dr. Holley had no white patients. He was quite prosperous, was married and had two young daughters. At first Sarah was impressed with the Holley family, but she soon learned that Mrs. Holley suffered from some psychological disorder, and thus Sarah's choice was narrowed to the household of the barber, Mr. William T. Dixie.

The choice was a fortunate one. Sarah Louise was an aristocrat, not in fact but in mind and manner. She and Mrs. Dixie thus had much in common and the Dixie family fitted well Sarah's requirements for Annie's foster home. Lucille Dixie Palmer stated that though her parents were born before the Emancipation Proclamation neither of them was born of slave parents. William T. Dixie had migrated from Danville, Virginia, and was eight years old when slavery ended. His wife, Willie Belle, had migrated from Christianburg, Virginia. The two met and married after coming to Bramwell, where Mr. Dixie was the only barber in the town, and served only white clientele.

Though Mr. Dixie was perhaps not as prosperous as Dr. Holley, he was quite comfortable. He had built a house on four acres of hillside land he owned, and there he fixed up a room for Annie "in the big hall." The Dixies eventually had five children of their own, four boys and one girl. The daughter, Lucille, and Annie grew quite fond of each other. Lucille admired Annie's "grownupness," for Annie was ten years older than she. Each said that the other was the nearest to a sister she ever had.

Sarah and Mrs. Dixie got along well with the living arrangements on which they had agreed. They worked together for the benefit of all the children. At one point, Mrs. Spencer recalled, two of the Dixie children had typhoid (or measles). Sarah took it upon herself to concoct a cure, for the illness was very serious and the doctor seemed to be doing little good. She made a poultice of herbs, onions, and "things," and bound it around the little girl all the way up to the neck. Later she did the same for the other child, and soon the children showed remarkable improvement. "The doctor didn't know what to make of it." In general, both Sarah and Mrs. Dixie acted as sort of joint mother to all the children.

It did not take Annie long after moving from the mining community into the Dixie home to adjust to the town and to the Dixies, a charming couple whom she grew to love dearly. At first there was not very much to excite Annie's mind in the Dixie home or in the town. "A shiny little white girl [Elsie Brown], daughter of the hotel owner where my mother worked, was the only playmate I had. I don't remember any colored children around then," except for the small Dixie children. Elsie and her parents lived on the same street that passed the Dixies' house and she and Annie struck up a friendship early which lasted until both left the area for good. Elsie was herself an only child; so the two had much in common, including their inquisitive and active minds. Elsie and Annie spent a lot of time together "doing all sorts of things." They were together so frequently that the townspeople came to expect this companionship. Annie and Elsie would often slip off and go to the old reservoir to catch frogs or to watch the many moccasins swimming in the river. They knew it was dangerous to play around the reservoir or frolic along the river's bank where the snakes clustered, but both of them loved the out-of-doors and the adults never knew they were courting danger.

In the town Annie and Elsie would run, skip, and play along the streets or go into the town's restaurant for treats. In the restaurant they ordered anything they wanted and never paid any attention to money. They knew that when one ordered something one had to pay, so the two would come into the restaurant, place their orders, and then put twenty-five cents on the counter. "Nobody ever told us it cost twenty-five cents; we just put the quarter down." This was of course a white restaurant, but Annie never was barred from it. The townspeople indulged both girls; the whites treated Annie as they would one of their own. "Nobody ever *said* Negroes could not eat there"; so she did. The people of the town had a particular fondness for Annie, for not only was she a beautiful child, but she grew to be quite an attractive young woman whose beauty was complemented by her wit, intelligence, and manners.

Life in Bramwell with the Dixies was relatively free and easy for Annie. Mrs. Dixie did not have outside employment; she spent her time taking care of her home, her children, and Annie. Even when Annie was old enough to do minor chores, Mrs. Dixie always excused her and never asked her to cook, sew, wash, or perform any other household tasks that most young girls between six and twelve are taught to do. She was left relatively free to do what she pleased, and "frilly things and chores" were not really to her liking, except on occasions when she wanted a change from her usual activities.

Lucille Dixie Palmer stated that she adored Annie, and that Mrs. Dixie often would have to say "stop looking at Annie," for Lucille would sit and stare in admiration. Since Annie was the older, Lucille admired that freedom she associated with age. One thing she particularly admired about Annie for quite some time was that Annie was old enough to do the things which were forbidden Lucille, such as wearing grown-up looking clothes.

Sarah dressed Annie in the best fashions of the day and with the most expensive taste, according to both Mrs. Palmer and Mrs. Spencer. Still enjoying the semblance of aristocracy, Sarah would order clothes, shoes, and trinkets from the best stores in New York. On several occasions she ordered Annie's shoes from I. Miller's on Fifth Avenue, at a price of four dollars and more—and in the nineteenth century, said Mrs. Spencer, this was expensive for children's shoes. But this was Sarah's way of giving her daughter the best life she could. No child in Bramwell, Mrs. Spencer maintained, was attired more expensively than she. Mrs. Spencer said that she realized more fully in later years that what she needed then was not expensive clothes but a home and a father. Even then she was somewhat indifferent to the cost of her clothes, but valued all her possessions simply because they were hers.

In spite of all the elaborate dresses and "frills," Annie was a tomboy. No doubt this irritated Sarah no end, for her pride was in trying to give Annie all the material possessions that the young girls of rich white Bramwell families sported and thus, in Sarah's mind, making a model young lady of her. Mrs. Palmer stated that Mrs. Dixie and Sarah followed then what one might term a "Victorian" code of manners and decorum, and their endeavor was to make Annie a model child patterned after what an affluent young white girl from one of the best families of the time (at least in Bramwell) would be. But Annie's mind was on things other than being a parlor princess.

She loved the out-of-doors and enjoyed running through the grass, collecting wild flowers, listening to the sounds of animals, and sitting on the river bank alone, just thinking and looking and listening. As she remembered it, "From the very beginning [Bramwell] was a lonely place. But Aunt Daisy—she was an outdoor person—would take me and her children for long 'tramps' in the woods." Annie began here to develop her love for and knowledge of the out-of-doors. She liked to work, and the more laborious the work, the better she liked it. Mrs. Palmer recalled that on many occasions, probably when neither Mrs. Dixie nor Sarah was around, Annie would shed her nice clothes —or sometimes keep them on—and do some very grimy work. She would take the notion to scrub the outhouse or paper it with the Sears catalog; or she would run frantically through the yard and fields, playing all sorts of games and doing the kind of things a tomboy would do. These impulsive bursts of activity contrasted sharply with the times when she was very serene and still, the times when she would just look and listen and think.

The outhouse was one of Annie's favorite places, for there she could have that undisturbed solitude which she seemed to cherish at times. Once she was barely learning to read, the outhouse became her haven. She would go there often and just read—"or pretend to read"—and would be very perturbed if anyone disturbed her in her hideaway. She was a gregarious child who enjoyed playing (especially with Elsie) when she was in the mood; but when she was in the mood for solitude and could not appropriate the outhouse, she found some other isolated place where she would just think or plug away at her new-found though confusing pastime—trying to read.

To the delight of the Dixie children, Annie at times displayed her theatrical talent. She thought it great fun to dramatize characters both from the stories she had heard Mrs. Dixie read to the children and from the ones she had tried to read. She liked pretending to be different people in different places and in different situations. She would cut out dolls from the Sears catalog for puppet shows and dramatize the stories she would tell the Dixie children. More often, when Mrs. Dixie was out of the house or away on some errand, Annie would dress up in Mrs. Dixie's clothes—or some other grown-up lady's clothes—and pretend to be a grownup, imagining herself to be some of those people in the stories she had read and heard. When she got tired of playing the role of grown-up lady, she would dress in Mr. Dixie's clothes and assume another character. Since the Dixie children were taught at home by their mother until they were old enough to be sent away to private school, they were home most of the time, and Annie's shows provided them with welcome and entertaining diversions. And after she learned to read well enough to get the gist of a story on her own, these diversions became more frequent. Her paper doll puppet shows developed into more human dramas, to the delight of the Dixie children. At times her performances required going through several costume changes. At other times she would coax the children into playing some of the parts. These little dramas became cherished pastimes for all the children in the Dixie household.

Of more importance, these little dramas sparked in Annie an urgent desire to read with ease. As in her adult life, Mrs. Spencer as a child had that independence of mind which made her want to do things her own way and with her own powers. She was not satisfied with merely hearing the stories read by Mrs. Dixie; she wanted to read them herself. Mrs. Dixie read often, and Annie would mimic her reading—most likely as part of her pretending to be the grown-up Mrs. Dixie when she would dress in the lady's clothes, for this was the "dramatic" period in her youth.

The reading materials in the Dixie home consisted of what Mr. Dixie brought home from his barber shop: mainly popular dime novels, newspapers, and the *Police Gazette*. They had no pictures (maybe a few sketches), but Annie, though she could not read, would "handle" them and pretend she read. The few books in her barber shop library which had any pictures at all had those "horrible pictures of naked women; looked like they —women—do walking up the street today." She began to "handle" the books and papers even before she pretended to read them. Often while playing in the house she would pick up the books and papers and look through them, partly out of curiosity and partly out of a desire for some diversion.

Mrs. Dixie was an avid reader and devoured the reading matter her husband brought home. Before long, Annie was "reading right along with her." Somehow, probably initially with the help of Mrs. Dixie, she learned to read a few of the words from the books; later she could "recognize sentences" and after some time she could "read" parts of the books and papers. "I cut my literary teeth on this stuff; yes, *this* is where I cut my literary teeth," she recalled.

By the time Mr. Dixie brought the books and magazines home from his barber shop, the backs and outside covers were torn away. Annie seldom if ever saw the covers, titles, or first and last pages of the materials that comprised her barber shop library. She recalled having seen the name of Laura Jean Libbey affixed to several of the books; yet even these books had no backs. "The novels people read then were not like the ones we read now. Most of Miss Libbey's novels were of 'the true story stuff'—melodrama. But I've always remembered her novel *He Loved But Was Lured Away*," Mrs. Spencer said.

Annie's first efforts in learning to read were sporadic, but she did not find her "instruction" on these limited occasions difficult to master. She had quite a good memory and a knack for learning. Even as a very young child she had a large vocabulary. "I was a bright child in the mouth. They made a lot over it: 'listen at the words that child uses.'" Such comments pleased Sarah immensely. Sarah herself always was eager to add new and "big" words to her own vocabulary, all as a part of the role she had assigned herself to play. Though she could hardly be said to be literate, her speech was almost perfect and one could not tell from the way she spoke that she had no formal education. Yet, Mrs. Spencer said, Sarah practically always misused the verb "to come" by saying "have came." "Mother was the most literate unlettered person I have ever known," said Mrs. Spencer.

Precocity, a good memory, and a large vocabulary were admirable in a child of nine or ten, but these could not compensate for a lack of more formal academic training. There were free schools for black children in the area at the time, but Annie remained at home. She easily could have attended the free school on the outskirts of Bramwell, but "Mother was an excellent snob." The students at the free school were primarily children of miners, and Sarah did not want Annie attending school with these children from families in a lower economic stratum. Mrs. Spencer never forgot one irony of the situation: a miner's son surnamed Taylor who attended the free school to which her mother refused to send her grew up to become very prosperous and ultimately became private secretary to a prominent person (perhaps an American ambassador) in Rome.

Sarah, however, would not subordinate her pride and belief in class distinctions to Annie's educational needs. She rejected the free school and did all she could at home to nurture Annie's knack for learning. Mrs. Spencer remembered that Sarah bought her *The Child's Picture Story of the Bible*, a book with many pictures but few words. Yet after Annie learned to "read" it, she could more easily plow through the dime novels and the *Police Gazette*. But of course Sarah's ability to teach Annie was limited in that she herself could read very little.

Mrs. Spencer recalled that "Sarah Louise could read reading [printed page] but couldn't read writing [script or handwriting]." Annie's curiosity about the printed page soon exceeded Sarah's ability to elucidate it for her, as is the case in this instance recorded in the Notebooks:

When I read the princess entered the ballroom on the arm of the

French Minister, I thought he had back-slid from the church to the point where he'd completely fallen from grace.

When I asked my mother to explain this: "Just what it says. I don't put no sort of doings pass big white folks—or little ones." Now that one sort of brainwash angle in what one way or the other is the reason why what you don't know does hurt you. You'll eventually read for the helpful doubt, if the art ever [advances] to that point. For the fight for literacy must begin to be facile enough to know that the prune & [prism?] ability to call every word in your language correctly may not be the ability to read—in any sense save a kind of switch-tail talent for show. The precise elocution of the *Delsarte Movement*[6] passed out even before its Boston protagonist died.

[Notebooks]

When Annie grew old enough so that it was obvious that she needed as well as desired teaching beyond what she could receive at home, Sarah mentioned this problem in one of her letters to Joel. Joel was upset that Annie was now about eleven years old and not enrolled in school; he pressed Sarah to enroll her right away. "[I] was the battleground on which they continued to fight out their distaste for each other: 'Put her in school!' 'She shall *never* go to school in a mining town!' So until I was 11 years old I'd never been in a school room" (Notebooks). Sarah still shunned the free schools and Joel finally issued an ultimatum: "He would come and take me back to Illinois with him, and the law would let him."

Joel's ultimatum caused Sarah even more concern, but a solution to the problem soon presented itself. During a church service Sarah heard a speaker address the congregation about a coeducational institution for blacks located in Lynchburg, Virginia. The man was traveling throughout the area to promote the school and gain students and support for it, Mrs. Spencer recalled. He mentioned how Virginia Seminary (organized and known as Lynchburg Baptist Seminary until 1890) was a self-

6. Mrs. Spencer's use of *Delsarte Movement* here refers to the term Delsarte system, a system of calisthenics attributed to the French teacher François Delsarte (1811–1871). What she intends by the metaphor is that her verbal calisthenics, her attempts at "precise elocution" without substantial understanding of what she was reading, were abandoned before the novel ended.

help school for Negroes and had been established to help bring education to black youth in the region. Lynchburg was not an unreasonable distance from Bramwell, and Virginia Seminary seemed just the place for Sarah to send Annie—for several reasons. Annie was blossoming into quite a beautiful young lady and Sarah never wanted her to be raised around white men. Bramwell's population was almost all white. Annie would have been vulnerable to illicit solicitations from white men who—if we are to believe historians and sociologists of the period—would have had rather free rein to make her a mistress. Given the particular culture at the time, Sarah's fears in this case are readily understandable. In addition, the seminary was a private school and its students—at least the majority of them—came from prominent black families of a class acceptable to Sarah. Finally, the cost of the boarding school was reasonable and Joel agreed to send ten dollars each month to pay Annie's expenses at the seminary. It cost eight dollars per month, but Sarah could use the extra two dollars and Joel was none the wiser. When Sarah left Joel she rejected everything associated with him—even his name. This is probably one of the very few times that she accepted anything from him that did not go directly to Annie.

In the summer of 1893 Sarah was busy making preparations for Annie's move to Lynchburg. "Mother had a friend there in Bramwell who wrote the letter to the Seminary and negotiated. The return letter was depressing because it said that they could only take children of twelve years old." Annie was eleven then and would not be twelve until February of the coming year, but Sarah was determined not to lose this opportunity to solve her problems. "Mother had about fifty dollars. She dressed me up and took me down to Lynchburg. Mother, too, looked very nice when we went down." She talked with the school's administrators and they agreed to admit Annie. Mrs. Spencer said she entered the seminary at eleven years old and they recorded her age as twelve and asked no questions. Sarah paid twenty-four dollars for three month's room, board, and instruction. "She left

Lynchburg and went to the [Chicago] World's Fair in September, 1893. For six years I remained their controversial student."

It may be useful to point out here the general significance of these early years in relation to Mrs. Spencer's young adulthood, to her mature life, and, most importantly, to her poetry. Her years at Virginia Seminary were to nurture, enrich, and perpetuate a personality and life-style which slowly but definitely had been forming during the five or six years she lived in Bramwell, a personality and a philosophy of life which come out clearly in the poetry of her adult years. These pre-seminary years were formative ones.

One notable aspect of her early years was her isolation from a peer group. She could recall her life as far back as age three, but she mentioned only one instance of playing with other children while living with her parents in the Martinsville, Virginia, area; never did she relate to me any sense of her family living and participating in a social community during these years. Until she was about six years old Annie was virtually alone in her childhood world in southwestern Virginia. Her human contacts were primarily with adults: at home with her mother and in Joel's bar. Being constantly and almost exclusively around adults apparently accounted for her early grasp of an adult-like vocabulary and for that precocity, wit, and intelligence noticeable when she was six or seven years old. She apparently came into contact with other children while living for a few months with Mrs. Clark in Winston-Salem; but this experience was short-lived, and her first extended contact with other children was after she came to Bramwell. But even in Bramwell she wasn't with children of her own age, for even the oldest of the Dixies' children was several years younger than Annie. Her cousins in the Bramwell area might have been in her age group, but they lived in the mining communities outside town and were seldom if ever her daily playmates. In fact, Sarah was not receptive to a very close relationship with her brother Nathan's family. "Now in West Virginia, I would go down to Uncle Nat's to play with his four children, [Neida?], Gertrude, Milton, and young Nathan. But she [Sarah] wouldn't let me stay with them because they looked like common, ordinary [people]. They didn't have napkins on the table, and didn't have so and so." Since her mother would not allow her to attend the school for black children in Bramwell, her contact with other children was even further limited. If there were black children of the domestic and service workers in Bramwell, Sarah's and Mrs. Dixie's class consciousness prevented them from establishing neighborly contacts with these families. In fact, Mrs. Spencer could not remember any black children in the town except the Dixies.

Annie's close friendship with Elsie Brown and her association with other whites in Bramwell conditioned her against accepting an inferior status in society assigned on the basis of race. Her introduction to overt racism came after she went to Lynchburg, a time when she was mature enough to recognize racial discrimination and to understand its practices and consequences. Her life in Bramwell had sheltered her from racial hatred, and it is to Bramwell that one can trace the roots of her philosophy "not to love or hate by color" or social status. In Bramwell she had learned to react to human beings as people, regardless of their color. Her free and easy movement through the town, the almost doting attention she received from the whites there, her independence of mind, and that pride in self which Sarah had inculcated in her must have led to a tumultuous reaction when in Lynchburg she was introduced to the realities of southern life in the late nineteenth century. But she did not alter her positive sense of self. The standards by which she had learned to measure her relationships with others remained intact; the southern way of life in terms of race and class distinctions did not claim her as one of its participants. The consequence was that she later developed a fervent indignation for those whites who practiced racial discrimination, and a contempt for those blacks who seemed to accept complacently the inferior status in life arbitrarily assigned to them.

In addition to her isolation from a peer group (until she went to Virginia Seminary), other circumstances of Annie's life in

Bramwell were conducive to a certain amount of psychological distancing from other people. Seriously disturbed over her parents' separation, Annie remained in the Dixie household with something less than total acclimation to the situation. She was not an adopted child, and always was aware that she was living in a foster home. From the beginning she was extremely fond of the Dixies, but this household never could replace the family unit composed of her own parents. This does not mean that there was ever any friction between Annie and anyone in the Dixie family—quite the contrary—but that by this time Annie's life with her parents had caused her to begin to develop a physical and psychological independence that was fostered by the circumstances of her life in Bramwell.

The seeds of personal freedom—psychological, intellectual, physical, emotional—were firmly planted and nourished during these years and matured during the ensuing years into that defiance, determination, independence, and self-esteem which were the essence of her life and writings. By choice she remained both a solitary and a gregarious person. Since the Bramwell days her life was characterized by few intimate contacts, but intense contacts in a one-to-one relationship. Ever since her friendship with Elsie the word "friend" held a special meaning for her, and defined her relationship with certain other people in her life, such as her husband, or James Weldon Johnson, or her Lynchburg friend, Bernice Lomax Hill. It is not surprising, therefore, that the term "friend" is central to many of her poems and indicative of a personal kinship which transcends the usual meaning of the term.

2 ✄ Education

After she left Joel, Sarah reassumed her maiden name of Scales. She did not want her daughter to have anything associated with Joel, especially his name; so it was under the name Annie Bethel Scales that she registered Annie at Virginia Seminary in Lynchburg in September, 1893. The fee was then eight dollars per month, though Mrs. Spencer remembered that later there were additional charges. At one point she had to pay another three dollars monthly for "pills" (medical care), for breakage in chemistry lab, and for foreign language instruction.

The seminary held school eight months a year. At that time its two divisions of study were academic and normal. The normal division was divided into three sections: middle normal, junior normal, senior normal. (Mrs. Spencer used various terms to characterize the academic levels at the school when she was a student there. These are the ones she used most frequently.) Annie was placed in the lowest middle normal section during her first term. Because she could barely read and write, the first few months, and perhaps the first few years, were difficult for her. She read little but pretended to read more. "When I went to the Seminary I could call all the words but couldn't understand them all." She had a lot of catching up to do. The natural and physical sciences always gave her trouble. In chemistry "I learned the words sulfuric acid and the stink and that's all." On the other hand, she had such motivation for the humanities that she soon excelled in those subjects. Once she acquired the rudimentary skills of reading and writing, she applied herself even more diligently to her studies. As the years progressed, Annie moved from the lowest sections of the normal divisions to most of the top sections for her class, becoming one of the highest achievers in the humanities courses. The best academic group studied the classics as a major part of its curriculum, Mrs. Spencer recalled. Though not enrolled in the academic division, Annie did have "three years of good basic Latin, one year of French and one year of German."

Living conditions at the seminary were substandard. That first year (and for all the years she spent there) Annie learned that one of the things students looked forward to was getting a box from home—more often than not containing food. "I loved the fried chicken, but it must have been putrid when it finally arrived. But we would share our home-cooked food." Inadequate food service was not the only problem the school faced in its early years of operation. The school itself was even younger than Annie, having opened in 1890 as Lynchburg Baptist Seminary, and was striving for survival; conditions of the physical plant in general were poor. "At the Seminary there was insufficient food; no plumbing," and generally bad conditions. "When I went home that [first] summer, I was sick." Dr. Griffin (in Bramwell) said that she had contracted malaria as a result of malnutrition. Sarah was appalled when she greeted Annie at the close of that first school year and saw the toll school life had taken on her. Yet the effect of the school was not enough to make Sarah withdraw her. She sent her back in the fall and tried to supplement the school's diet. "Mother would send me a box as often as she could after she saw me that first summer home."

Over the summer Annie regained some of the strength and vigor she had first taken to the seminary. With Dr. Griffin's care and Sarah's motherly attention, by fall she was ready to return to Lynchburg. Even as she left Bramwell the effects of her illness were noticeable, but shortly after returning to Lynchburg she became her vigorous self again and continued to progress rapidly in her studies.

"I was a tomboy for those first three years" at the seminary, she recalled. In those days "I was a good ball player. A girl hit me with a bat and I couldn't walk without pain for one whole term." If Annie did spend some of her time doing "tomboyish things," more often she applied her time to her studies, and her natural gift for learning became evident. "By the middle [preparatory years] I was the best reader in the class."

Her abilities caught the attention of Dr. Gregory W. Hayes, who was president of the seminary during the entire time Annie was there as a student. "He also taught Sunday school and made me his assistant Sunday school teacher." Dr. Hayes became so impressed with Annie's talent that he frequently asked her to take charge of his classes when he had to be away. "Dr. Hayes taught me arguments out of Hill's *Outline of Psychology*." Psychology was a new subject then for the students at Virginia Seminary. Mrs. Spencer remembered that she and most of the other students would sit awe-struck for entire class periods listening to Dr. Hayes lecture on psychology.

Annie eventually became a good friend of the young lady who was to marry Dr. Hayes. Mary Rice was one of about three women whom Annie considered almost as close as a sister. When Dr. Hayes and Mary Rice were married, they were given a honeymoon trip to Boston where he also transacted business for the seminary and tried to gain support for the striving school. Mrs. Spencer remembered that Dr. Hayes wanted to take a student along to show his potential supporters what kind of job the seminary was doing and why it should be given further support. He chose Annie to accompany them, and at first she was delighted. But on further reflection she realized that she did not have the proper clothes to make such a trip. It is obvious that as a budding young girl she now was getting out of her tomboyish ways and becoming more conscious of the latest fashions in dress, which she always had been used to but to which she had been somewhat indifferent. Understanding more clearly now her mother's situation, she would not ask her to provide the wardrobe to make such a trip. No doubt Sarah would have provided the most expensive attire, since she always had spent lavishly for Annie's normal everyday wear, but Annie regretfully declined the honored invitation and Dr. Hayes took another student, Annie's best friend, Youtha Black (who was disappointed in the trip).

Annie was one of Dr. Hayes's brightest pupils, and as she matured he told her some of the administrative problems the seminary faced. "The white Baptist Convention was giving the school one thousand dollars a year and required that certain things go on—like at Tuskegee—teaching trades, sewing, and so on." Administrators who were trying to maintain schools for blacks—especially those who were partially dependent on financial support from whites—had to do certain things that some of them would rather not have done. Annie learned from Dr. Hayes that this was the case at Virginia Seminary. Periodically the financial supporters, such as the white National Baptist Convention, sent representatives to inspect the school to determine what was going on, at which time the inspectors were shown exactly what they wanted to see: trades and industrial courses being taught. When the inspectors left, the school would exhume the briefly but conveniently buried Latin texts and literature books and decrease the number of sewing machines, ironing boards, and hammers. The typical though covert curriculum would continue, teaching "the workers to work and the thinkers to think," as W. E. B. Du Bois stated it.[1]

Mrs. Spencer's comments about the seminary here are closely connected with the controversy between Du Bois and Booker T. Washington at the turn of the century about the education of blacks. There was at that time a widespread tendency to follow the example of Washington's philosophy and teach black students primarily the trades. Many whites held the belief—to which many blacks acquiesced—that blacks did not need a liberal education or instruction in the arts and sciences, but instead needed to be taught salable skills in the industrial trades. But through "devious" means Annie Scales and many other black students at Virginia Seminary, as well as many students at black

1. W. E. B. Du Bois, *The Souls of Black Folk* (Chicago: A. C. McClurg and Co., 1903), 86. In Chapters 5 and 6 Du Bois presents part of his side of this controversy about the education of blacks. The entire issue is too complex to be outlined here, and one should consult various histories on this issue.

institutions throughout the country, acquired instruction in the liberal arts.

On at least one occasion, however, the seminary was "caught" teaching its students liberal arts. Mr. McVickers, head of the National Baptist Convention, often visited the seminary to ascertain how things were being done. "He saw them teaching Greek, and so on, and didn't like it. He made a speech in the Chapel [to faculty and students] on one of the occasions while he was visiting, saying that Negroes had not arrived at the time when they needed to be taught Greek and Latin. He took away the one thousand dollars the Seminary was receiving from the National Baptist Convention. The thousand dollars went directly to Dr. Hayes because they [the seminary] had no money to pay him. Dr. Hayes refused to give in. He refused to stop teaching academic subjects. He gave up the money."

The teachers at the seminary, blacks and some whites, were excellent. They were graduates of Colgate, the University of Pennsylvania, Temple University, New York University, and other noted schools. Mrs. Spencer remarked that the North would educate these young people and then refuse to give them jobs. "So they came to the South to get experience, certainly not to get money." She remembered that her teachers were given room and board and twenty-five or thirty dollars (top pay) per month. They were intelligent and gifted young teachers, and they made quite an impression on Annie. "What education I have, I guess I got it there. Surely I got what enlightenment I have there," Mrs. Spencer reflected.

Mrs. Spencer believed that her teachers enlightened her more than they taught her. She believed that after the tenth grade a child can learn for himself, if he has any intelligence at all. She was not book-oriented, and cared little for regurgitating facts on examinations. She said that there is a difference between learning (repeating what one has been told) and enlightenment. Too often "we give up wisdom trying to get knowledge," she maintained.

Annie's academic performance at the seminary was uneven.

Her teachers, in addition to Dr. Hayes (who, she said, taught her to look at literature as life), were no doubt aware of a certain gift she had for mastering courses in the humanities, but in her physical science courses Annie's performance was not impressive. Her grade average was too low to place her among the high academic achievers for her class. To help improve her grades in the sciences, Annie recruited a young man at the seminary, Edward Spencer. "He helped me with my geometry and I translated his Caesar." Edward was six years older than Annie. By sharing homework, the two became close friends. "This is where and how I met my husband," she said.

Not long after Annie enrolled at the seminary, she was asked to take "love notes" from the older coeds to their young men on campus. "Then one day I decided not to. I started looking at boys for my own eyes. Before, [the coeds] would say, 'isn't she sweet,' or 'isn't she cute,' and so on," while she was delivering their notes. "After I stopped, I was despised." "Courting" was done in a very Victorian manner at the school then. "You would see your 'sweetheart' downstairs at a social once a month." Otherwise, one would have to admire from afar and hope none of the authorities at the seminary noticed that he was breaking a very strict social rule.

The enrollment at the school was small and students could not help noticing one another. Annie had noticed Edward Spencer, but because he was older and was sporting with the older girls, she at first had few or no amorous hopes. But Edward had been making an impression on her for a long time with his hearty attitude toward other students. "There was no plumbing or central heating at the Seminary. A young man would draw water from the school well for his special girl. You could do a lot more bathing then with a quart of water! Pop [Edward] would stay by the well and draw water for girls without a beau." This gallant practice clinched it. "I made my selection then and worked toward it."

The first young man at the seminary to openly express romantic interest to Annie was an "arrogant, conceited boy" named

Jack Vaughn. He began by writing her several love notes. She never answered any of them, but each of his succeeding letters would be composed as though Annie not only had answered the previous ones but had answered them favorably. She burned the letters and ignored the young man. Finally, realizing the futility of his pursuit, he asked her to return all his letters. She replied that she did not even know where the ashes were. This retort clipped Jack Vaughn's plume, she remembered. Edward Spencer, who probably had an eye for Annie all along and who witnessed this incident in class, proceeded to write her a note asking whether, if he wrote her love notes, she would treat him that way. She wrote a one-word reply in capital letters—TRY—and signed it "Hussy." Their relationship began to develop more concretely after this, for he did try and succeeded.

"A lot of things happened to me there at the Seminary when I was fourteen years old," Mrs. Spencer reflected. One of the many things was her grappling with religion. Sarah was a religious woman and had tried with some success to instruct Annie. She had used the Bible in her efforts to teach Annie to read before she sent her to school. "When I did start [to read] in the Bible I was wrapped up in the Old Testament." (Her first published poem, "Before the Feast at Shushan," is based on the Book of Esther.) Her contact with the Bible continued after she entered school, for the seminary had a fairly competent theological school and a large number of its students were theological students. "The young preachers [theological students] and I had bull sessions." Perhaps most of the other students took theological courses since the school was church affiliated, and Annie had ample occasion to engage in exercises of the mind.

In one theology class the students studied the psychology of religion. "This is how I learned about Kant. When something would come up to argue about, I'd go to the library and read all I could about it." By age fourteen Annie had made it a regular practice to discourse upon religious questions with her schoolmates. She would anticipate arguments and discussions with fellow students and then prepare herself beforehand by scrutinizing the Bible and other sources to make her side of the discussions stronger. What her opponents attributed to a remarkable skill with spontaneous answers was actually diligence; in general she acquired a good reputation with her fellow students and with her teachers.

One of the results of this argumentative skill was a growing doubt about biblical and religious matters, problems which she could not resolve in her discussions with her schoolmates. She reflected: "I disagreed with the religion being taught at the Seminary, and I wrote about going to hell. You see, when I was fourteen they had told me when I was twelve that I would have to be answerable for my sins. Did you ever hear that? Well, that was the folkism way back then. Just to think when I was twelve —and I'm ninety now. Well, I didn't want to have to answer [for my sins], so I wrote this little piece—it was sonnet form—called 'The Skeptic,' meaning that I don't believe it. That's the first poem I ever wrote in my life." The poem is now lost, but evidently this creative though juvenile activity eased her mind somewhat and began what since became a practice of expressing her inner thoughts in poetry. Recalling "The Skeptic" and the beginnings of this lifelong practice, she added: "When you're beginning to *think*, you think, you feel, you taste, you see, you smell; heretofore you've just been sniffing from the outside and touching. But when something boils up in you, you have thoughts that you've never had before."

Annie knew little about poetry and its forms when she wrote "The Skeptic." When I knew her she could not recall ever having read a sonnet before she wrote her poem. But she had read some forms of verse before 1896, mainly those verse pieces and rhymes written for children. "I had only read poems in McGuffey's *Reader*," she explained.

The summer of her fifteenth year was a memorable one. "That summer Mother thought I should be taught about my father and that situation." Annie never had understood clearly why the family broke up, nor had she resigned herself to it. She was particularly disturbed that she did not have her father's name and had written to him to ask why. He wrote back and said "your mother won't let you." Her mother's reply was, "I wouldn't let you go by that Negro's name."

Sarah told Annie several things about her past history and about the joys and troubles between herself and Joel. She focused on what Mrs. Spencer termed the "tragedy on the barroom floor." Of the many things they talked about that summer, this was the most memorable for Annie. When she returned to Virginia Seminary for her fifth year, she understood the family's history much better. The close and mature relationship which she developed with her mother that summer left Annie with a clearer understanding of Sarah's whole manner, though she cannot be said to have adopted many of Sarah's manners and attitudes.

This same summer was memorable to Mrs. Spencer for another reason. During her fourth year at the seminary Annie's roommate Pearl Matthews and her sister Clara asked Annie to spend part of the summer with them in Farmville, Virginia. "I had my first beau in Farmville, Virginia—Jack something— when I was fifteen. Girls had beaux in those days, not *a* beau. In those days a group of boys would go from house to house [on Sunday afternoons] to see the girls in their class." "Jack something" was from a well-to-do family in the Farmville area and periodically "came courting" that summer. He could afford the impressive luxury of taking his dates for rides in his fine buggy with a fringe on the top, Mrs. Spencer remembered. On Sundays Annie would dress up in her prettiest Sunday wear and Jack would pick her up. The two would ride in a wide circle a little distance from the house and then all—Jack, Annie, and the Matthewses—would go to the church services. But Jack's impression on Annie was negligible, for it was in this summer that her "match with Ed was sealed."

During that summer there was a big picnic scheduled in Farmville at Pickens' Farm. Sarah decided that the girls should have new dresses for the event. She bought the finest material and had dresses made for all three girls. Mrs. Spencer said that then she was sure that her dress, made from a red material which would look good only on certain girls, was the most beautiful and elaborate at the picnic. The picnic and following barn dance were successful. When she recalled the picnic and other black functions in general, and spoke of the separation of the races, Mrs. Spencer concluded: "We were sure whites were stupid—as we are now. We had our pleasures and didn't think of the whites—we certainly didn't envy them."

Several years later Annie was to remember this picnic for another reason: there she first met W. E. B. Du Bois.[2] "I had no idea who Du Bois was when I met him in Farmville. The title 'doctor' made me think that he was a medical doctor." When they met again, she mentioned this picnic to Du Bois and "he pretended to remember the girl in the beautiful red dress," for Annie and her elaborate dress had drawn admiring attention.

What Annie gained at the seminary helped shape significantly what she did and what she became. She progressed from a little girl of eleven who could barely read and write to a mature woman whose diligence in learning made reading and writing a cherished function of her life which she at times went to elaborate lengths to maintain.

Annie had worked hard during her six years at the seminary and had done extremely well in several courses. She had earned admiration and respect from many of her schoolmates and teachers. In the spring of 1899 Annie Bethel Scales, at seventeen, and Edward Spencer, at twenty-three, were preparing for graduation. The class valedictorian and salutatorian had been selected from the highest section of the academic division and were expected to give speeches at the graduation ceremony. Mrs. Spen-

2. This summer Du Bois traveled widely in the South and studied the economic situation of blacks in several small southern towns. This was between the time he left his job at the University of Pennsylvania in the spring and the time he assumed a position at Atlanta University in the fall of 1897. In 1898 he published a study titled "The Negroes of Farmville, Virginia" in the *Bulletin of the Department of Labor* (Washington, D.C.: Government Printing Office, 1898), III, 1–38. For further information see Herbert Aptheker (ed.), *The Correspondence of W. E. B. Du Bois: Volume I, Selections, 1877–1934* (Amherst: University of Massachusetts Press, 1973).

cer recalled that the young girl chosen valedictorian, Keziah Dyke, had a brilliant mind but her shyness made her delivery as a speaker somewhat strained. She was "one of those innocents," as Mrs. Spencer expressed it. The young man chosen as salutatorian was William Christian. Though William's academic performance had been superior, "he was a dull student." The teacher read his speech and remarked that he could make no sense of it, that every sentence seemed to waver. So Annie was asked to write a speech.

The assignment was a welcome challenge. Annie labored over her speech, using several of her own defiant and independent ideas and incorporating with them materials she had gleaned from numerous books she had read in the seminary's library. Part of the material for her speech she took from James Bryce's *The American Commonwealth* (1888); but most of the reference material came from the writings of Alexis de Tocqueville, chiefly his *Democracy in America* (1835–1839). "Bryce has a section called 'The Social Institution'[3] which textually makes the statement 'what is the future of the Negro.' But de Tocqueville says it will in the future be a big revolution (slave uprising or rebellion)." Speaking of black people's struggles since the days of slavery, Mrs. Spencer said "Virginia was the cause of all this revolution and de Tocqueville says so. He says also that Virginia [and/or slavery?] was the cause of the American Revolution; it wasn't Tea and Taxation, but the United States had these slaves." (In Volume I, Chapter XVIII, which deals with the three races in the United States, de Tocqueville states that a racial clash in the United States is inevitable. In Volume II, Book III, Chapter XXI, he states that "If ever America undergoes great revolutions, they will be brought about by the presence of the black race on the soil of the United States."[4]) When she finished her research and writing, Annie felt she had composed a forceful and illuminating essay.

3. James Bryce, *The American Commonwealth* (New York: Macmillan & Co., 1888). The chapter referred to is probably either "The Future of Political Institutions" or "Social and Economic Future."

4. Alexis de Tocqueville, *Democracy in America*, trans. Henry Reeve, ed. Francis Bowen (3rd. ed.; Cambridge: Sever & Francis, 1863), II, 313–15.

Mrs. Spencer affirmed that her speech was not one of those accommodating speeches that Negroes then might have given before an integrated audience (whites were at the ceremony); it dealt with the bare truth, with the plight of the Negro in the United States. She emphasized in it that "if any disposition is to be made of the Negro, we will make that disposition." In reference to this speech Mrs. Spencer said that the concept of black power expressed in the 1960s and 1970s was "not a new thing," that she and others expressed it in the 1890s and that the concept had been expressed before her time. In fact, many years later one of her daughters delivered the same speech at her own graduation and several people, including officials of the board of education, requested copies of it. Unfortunately, all copies have now been lost. The instructor was so pleased with "Through Sacrifice to Victory" that he asked Annie to deliver the speech at the graduation exercises.

The graduating class, faculty, and administrators took the train to Lexington, Virginia, a town not far from Lynchburg, where on May 8, 1899, Virginia Seminary held its graduation exercises at Diamond Hill Baptist Church. "Pop [Edward Spencer] sang baritone; I gave the valedictory—unjustly." This was an "honor" Mrs. Spencer said she always regretted. The names of those students receiving highest honors in both the normal and academic divisions were printed on the graduation program. Since she was to deliver the major student address for the normal division, Annie Scales's name was given top honor on the program and the name of Keziah Dyke, the young lady who was supposed to deliver the valedictory, was included in the list of undistinguished graduates. Mrs. Spencer felt that this was not only misleading but unjust; she took no pride in it.

"Things were switched at that time," Mrs. Spencer related. Instead of blacks being in the balcony of the church where the ceremonies were held, whites were in the balcony and blacks were on the main floor. Among the whites in the balcony were students from Washington and Lee University and Virginia Military Institute, and maybe some other schools in the area. Annie Scales delivered her speech with poise and force, and several people from the audience later complimented her on a job well done. (Even in her last year of life, when she had reason to recall it, Mrs. Spencer assumed a remarkable teenage attitude as she recited lines from her speech. It was not difficult to imagine her as seventeen again—her hair bobbing in braids and her face showing a kind of innocent determination.) A day or so after the ceremony Annie received a bouquet of flowers from two young men from Washington and Lee University who had been impressed by her speech. Mrs. Spencer loved to recall her first bouquet. She also remembered that the bouquet did not go unnoticed by both blacks and whites in the town.

The bouquet of flowers was not the only gift Annie received for her graduation. She remembered that Dr. Richard H. Bolling, then head of a Negro Baptist publishing company in Nashville, Tennessee, gave her two presents for graduation: five dollars and, later, a copy of the finest Bible the company put out. She kept and read that same Bible for the rest of her life. Some time after her graduation "Dr. Bolling sent me a four-volume set of Emerson, which I still have. Dr. Bolling also gave me a philosophy which I cherished: 'Take what you have and make what you want.'" (This maxim has close affinity to her philosophy of life expressed in "Substitution.")

Annie graduated from Virginia Seminary without the presence of either of her parents. Sarah Louise was ill and could not make the trip. Annie sent Joel an invitation—"hopeful"—but he did not come. It had been about thirteen years since she had been taken away from her father, and once she and Sarah left Martinsville they apparently never saw Joel again. After he went to Illinois, he never came to the South again, Mrs. Spencer said. According to her, Joel had a job in Illinois that made him feel he was not a hired hand, as he always had felt in the South. "The day we graduated my father doubled the ten dollars per month and made it twenty dollars. My father sent ten dollars *then*; *now*, that would be one hundred dollars Nixon money. After Mother left him he never sent one cent unless it was connected with me." Though Annie probably never saw her father again, they did correspond after she went to the seminary and learned to write. Shortly after arriving there, she wrote to him asking for enough money to buy a bicycle. In Joel's reply he asked what she wanted with a bicycle when she could not even count. Bicycles then cost ten or fifteen dollars, Mrs. Spencer recalled.

Annie's graduation speech affected more whites than the two young men who sent her the bouquet. On the return trip from Lexington to Lynchburg after the graduation ceremonies, Annie struck up a conversation with a white lady, Mrs. Alexander Embree, who had heard her speech. (This particular train line between Lynchburg and Lexington was not segregated.) The brief conversation was full of congratulatory comments on Annie's "fine speech." Mrs. Embree asked for her address and some time later Annie received a card from her. "She told me, 'you gave me things to think about.'"

3 🎵 Marriage

The summer following her graduation Annie returned to Bramwell, as she had done each summer while attending the seminary. During the summer of 1899 she "just lived with the Dixies and did what they did and wrote Ed." By this time she had become more than "quite attached" to Edward, and perhaps this summer she was not as eager to leave Lynchburg as in the past. But before long Edward too had left Lynchburg and gone north, where he was hired to work on a buffet car which ran between New York and Montreal. "That's where he made his first money." Between graduation and their next meeting, a year later, Edward wrote Annie long letters—one stretching to forty-two pages. He knew she loved books and so he sent her "books and things" during the year and wrote a lot about his experiences on his new job. To keep his image fresh in her mind during this absence, as a birthday gift he sent her a large portrait.

Toward the end of the summer Annie began to think seriously about securing a job. For the most part, educated young blacks at the turn of the century in the South were limited to the professions of teaching and preaching; educated young black women had their choice of a profession even further narrowed. So, like most graduates of black normal schools at that time, Annie sought a teaching position. The salary for a black teacher in Virginia was twenty-five dollars per month for first grade teachers, Mrs. Spencer remembered, while in West Virginia it was forty-five dollars. Since there was practically no choice about what kind of work she could find and where she should work, she began to look for a teaching position in the Bramwell area. Yet her credentials from the seminary did not qualify her to teach in West Virginia, and she was required to take a certification examination. The test posed few problems, being primarily a test of knowledge in traditional academic subjects. Mrs. Spencer remembered that while at work on the test she noticed a young white man, one of the monitors for the examination, had stopped by her seat and was looking over her shoulder. She was pondering a question on Russian history, changing her answer from Catherine I to Catherine II and back again. Becoming slightly nervous with the man looking over her shoulder, she wrote Catherine I for the answer and hastily proceeded to the next question. The young man looked at the answer, pointed to the question and said "Peter the Great," and then moved on. Annie changed her answer to Peter the Great. She later thought about this incident so often that she developed an interest in Peter the Great and read widely about him.

Annie passed the state certifying test, but she was required to take a six-week workshop for teachers. After completing the workshop, she got a job teaching second grade in Maybeury, West Virginia. Maybeury was more a community or settlement than a town and was too far from Bramwell for her to commute each day. She secured lodging with a local family there and returned to Bramwell to spend weekends with the Dixie family and her mother. From the beginning she did not particularly like Maybeury and looked forward to the end of the school term. She had "a bad experience with a man" who was a relative of the couple who owned the rooming house where she lived, and this helped shorten her stay in Maybeury. Supported by his relatives, the man made advances and proposals, and when Annie shunned them he called her "finicky and stuck up." He "pestered" her for quite some time, and on her weekends in Bramwell she complained to her mother and the Dixies about her living situation in Maybeury. Annie's frequent talks with Mrs. Dixie about the total situation and her growing fear of this man gained her a sympathetic ear, and Mrs. Dixie finally supported Annie's desire to leave Maybeury. A few inquiries were made and Annie learned of a teaching position in Elkhorn, another small community in the Bramwell-Maybeury area. She willingly accepted the advice of Mrs. Dixie and she made the transfer to Elkhorn and finished out her teaching year, following the same pattern of spending the weekends in Bramwell.

Annie Scales made forty-five dollars a month teaching school in West Virginia (she remembered that her principal made sixty); since the communities of Maybeury and Elkhorn were probably under the same administrative agency, there was not even an interruption in her pay when she transferred to Elkhorn. The school year there lasted about eight months, ending about March (or May?) 15, Mrs. Spencer recalled. Dr. Hayes, still president of the seminary, asked her to come to the Lynchburg area and teach school during the West Virginia spring-summer school break. Since there was no position available in Lynchburg when she arrived, she was given a position in Naola, a community just north of Lynchburg. Several families or persons in the Naola area "took teachers"—which meant that theirs were nice, respectable, and usually comfortable homes—and Annie found lodgings with a Miss Jefferson. She taught in a "big log cabin school with three rooms on each side" of the main or central structure. "We had no privy built there. That was my masterpiece." Amazed that no one had taken the initiative to provide sanitary facilities for the students, she designed a privy, which was built over a small stream that ran near the school. The facility turned out to be quite an example of rural ingenuity in plumbing. The summer school term over for her in Naola, she perhaps returned to Elkhorn for one more year of teaching (though she said little about that second year in the Bramwell area after her graduation). In a short autobiographical sketch dated November, 1959, Mrs. Spencer mentioned her teaching experience in the Bramwell area: "Skip two county winters except to say we loved each other, the children I was supposed to know enough to teach, and I. They taught me the beginning of woodlore, and that hot spicewood tea was delicious. We had spelling bees, and charades, and pieces to speak—long ones."[1]

1. Spencer Family Papers, Anne Spencer House and Garden Historic Landmark, Lynchburg, Virginia.

With the problem of a career, or at least a job, seemingly settled now, Annie's attention turned to marriage—to Edward Spencer. "Mother was always trying to get me married off." And though Sarah was aware of the bond between Annie and Edward, he was not at the top of Sarah's list of prospective husbands for Annie. As far as Sarah was concerned, Edward's "profession" did not recommend him for the match, and she tried at least twice to promote marriages between Annie and the more affluent blacks in Bramwell. Dr. Holley, Bramwell's only black doctor, was fairly well off economically, considering the status of blacks in Bramwell at the time. "Dr. Holley went to Mother and asked for my hand in marriage." This was when Annie was seventeen. Sarah was quite impressed and enthusiastic, but Annie was not very receptive to this proposal. She loved Edward, and Dr. Holley, much older than she, had two daughters near Annie's age, as well as a wife, though she was in an asylum. Sarah argued that Dr. Holley was in the process of getting a divorce and, among other things, that he lived in an attractive little English-looking house he had built. Evidently Sarah was impressed by the prestige of this particular match, but "Mrs. Dixie layed Mother out for being taken in by Holley, for after all he had a wife already in the insane asylum."

Another of Sarah's prospects was a man whom Annie characterized as "the Walrus." "The Walrus" was principal of a school and came calling on Annie on more than one occasion after her seventeenth birthday. On what turned out to be the last of these "courting" visits, Annie was upstairs in her room when he arrived. She was summoned down to take company, but shunned all pretenses, knowing that the ultimate intention was marriage. "The Walrus" waited patiently downstairs and made polite conversation, but Annie still refused to heed her summons. Instead, she decided to "escape." Mrs. Spencer recalled that there usually was a ladder at her window (had she tried this route of escape before?), and she decided to take the ladder down and escape into the yard and disappear for a while, hoping "the Walrus" would leave. She went to the window and discovered to her frustration and anger that the ladder had been removed.

But this did not deter her determination not to be subjected to sweet parlor talk with the intention of being married off to a man whom she neither loved nor liked. The only way to escape now was to jump from the window. She did jump; but she did not escape. If the people gathered in the sitting room did not hear her fall, they surely heard her screams, for on her jump she sprained both ankles, "which haven't been right since." "The Walrus" was indeed sorry that his pursuit had caused such an accident. In the past he had insisted that Annie would be better off marrying him, and often spoke of Edward Spencer condescendingly as "that porter boy Annie is going to throw herself away on." But after the accident "the Walrus," realizing that Annie had little or no affection for him and that his pursuit had caused her undue pain, apologized for the trouble he had caused and never came back again. Apparently all of Sarah's efforts for match-making ceased after this incident, but her objections to Edward as her future son-in-law continued.

Annie's intentions remained firm. As a young adult she exercised an independence of mind that was to be a characteristic of her entire life. Edward Spencer was from a working-class family and, I gather, not as economically and socially mobile as many other students at the seminary. Mrs. Spencer mentioned how Jack Vaughn and others of her friends and beaux at the seminary could not understand why she was attracted to Edward instead of to them, and some of her associates in Bramwell at first looked askance at Edward and thought that Annie's attraction to a person who was not of their class was somewhat out of order. Such condescending attitudes did more to seal her relationship with Edward than to sever it; her personal likes and dislikes would not be dictated.

I would suspect that some who discouraged Annie's relationship with Edward did so for reasons other than Edward's modest economic standing. And though Mrs. Spencer never said this directly, Sarah's initial rejection of Edward as her prospective son-in-law probably had as much to do with his color as with his economic background and future prospects. Judging from his pictures, Edward was not a bright mulatto. And Mrs. Spencer implied more than once that intraracial color prejudice often characterized Sarah's dealings with blacks shades darker than she.

But Annie was and remained her own person. Partly out of defiance of those who disapproved of her association with Edward, she allowed her love for him to develop. Her open-minded attitude toward people throughout her adolescent and adult life, regardless of race, color, caste, or class, seems a direct outgrowth of her early life in Bramwell where she never was a victim of racial or social discrimination.

Certainly by May of 1901 everyone accepted the fact that Annie would make her own decision about whom she would marry and that that choice would be Edward Spencer. Edward and his brother Warwick came to Bramwell and prepared for the wedding in mid-May. The date of the Spencers' marriage has always been recorded as May 17 because Edward Spencer thought for some reason that the actual date of their marriage (Friday, May 15) was unlucky. However, it was on May 15, 1901, that Annie Bethel Scales and Edward Alexander[2] Spencer were married by the Reverend Frank Marshall in Bramwell, West Virginia, in the home of Mr. and Mrs. Dixie. Annie Scales had five dollars and ten cents when she married Edward Spencer: "that was my trousseau." What she did bring to the marriage was a love that lasted long after Edward's death (compare her poem "I Have a Friend"). The evening of their marriage Annie and Edward Spencer left Bramwell for Lynchburg, Virginia, and it was several months before she visited Bramwell again.

Setting up housekeeping in Lynchburg, the young couple lived for a short time in the "old home" area at 1804 Holiday Street, the street where Edward Spencer's parents had lived for many years, and the same street on which he was born. Within three years the family had grown to include two daughters,

2. Actually, Edward's middle name was not Alexander. He was named Edward Boyd Spencer, but when he entered the seminary he changed it to E. A.—Edward Alexander, after Alexander the Great.

Bethel Calloway and Alroy Sarah. Edward had spent his time during these four years building a home and establishing security and allowing Annie freedom in her own domain. A third child was born to the family, a son who died of diphtheria eleven hours after birth. "We intended to name him John." In 1903 Edward and Annie and their two daughters moved to the home Edward had built in the "Camp Davis" area in Lynchburg, 1313 Pierce Street, and here their last child was born, a son, Chauncey Edward.

Edward Spencer was a resourceful person and worked diligently to make the house on Pierce Street a home. Years later, his son wrote of him: "Dad first owned a grocery store with his brother; then he had a Post Office job, making a lucrative $1,000–$1,200 in 1910. They also made numerous investments in real estate, buying lots, 100 x 180, 'two for a quarter,' meaning two lots for twenty-five dollars." [3] After working at his regular jobs during the day, he would spend his evenings and weekends meticulously to improve the appearance and comfort of his home. He would pick up things here and there while traveling in and around the town and bring them home, where he usually was able to rehabilitate the objects and find some practical use for them around the house: "Ed was always picking up trash and making it look like it [could be insured by] Lloyd's of London."

The house on Pierce Street was small when the young couple moved there, but over the years Edward added stories and rooms and made other alterations. He would spend hours shaping metal, carving some piece of wood, and making "fancy" designs to enhance the beauty of the house. Visitors to 1313 Pierce Street still admire the intricately wrought copper-inlaid baseboards in the dining room and the mosaic mantel over the fireplace which contains in its colorful pattern lines from Mrs. Spencer's poems, as does a wall in the kitchen.

Edward worked hard and was successful in his practical aims,

3. Chauncey E. Spencer, *Who Is Chauncey Spencer?* (Detroit: Broadside Press, 1975), 13.

though "people didn't have much in those days." Mrs. Spencer recalled an anecdote to describe her husband's resourcefulness. "Nothing is destroyed in nature," she had on occasion repeated to her younger daughter Alroy. In class one day Alroy's chemistry teacher made the same statement, and Alroy innocently responded that she knew nothing was destroyed in nature because her father brought it home. In Mrs. Spencer's words, "Ed was the answer to his own prayer; he did the impossible." To further characterize his industrious nature, Mrs. Spencer recounted an interview with a group of local high school students who came to see her in the spring of 1972. One young girl in the group commented that all the rooms in the house were different. Mrs. Spencer replied: "Of course they are; Pop got them from all over the town."

Indeed, things were hard in those days, and for a black man things were even harder, Mrs. Spencer reflected. As a young housewife Annie had a certain amount of freedom (a term which had several meanings for Mrs. Spencer) that Edward did not have as head of a household. "The suppression of the Negro man has always existed until the present. Now they are beginning to be free and are showing the world their great worth. A man needs to be king at least of his own household, and a woman needs to be queen. They are getting free now, and it's a good thing."

During the early years of their marriage while Edward was working toward comfort and security for his family, Annie was caring for the children and spending many hours in the garden that Edward had built for her in the backyard. Annie was an avid gardener and housewife. But she had her own way of defining that: "I never washed or ironed a shirt for him; I'm not a housekeeper." All the same, she took great pleasure in her home and she and Edward worked together, even traveling many miles to acquire a rare plant to place in the garden. After some years the Spencers' garden became a noted sight in Lynchburg for its collection of varied plants and flowers, and for its well-tended form.

It was the garden and her writing that received most of Annie Spencer's time. Apart from a short term of teaching at Virginia Seminary (probably about 1911 or 1912) up until she began work at Dunbar High School Library, she enjoyed the life of leisure and reflection which her temperament required. She not only did not wash or iron a shirt, but she neither cooked nor cleaned unless she wanted to. There were always people to help with the domestic chores. Even before Mrs. Spencer's mother came to live with the family in the early 1920s, there was always someone to take care of the children, to do the house cleaning, to wash and to iron, to cook at times, and so on. Often there was more than one person in the Spencers' employment at one time. According to Chauncey Spencer, Mrs. Meekins and Mrs. Smith were among the ladies who came in daily to see that the children were given breakfast, dressed, and sent off to school, and that they were fed and cared for once they returned from school.

For a long time the Spencers hired a lady to do the family's washing who was so admired that more than once she is the subject of an entry in Mrs. Spencer's Notebooks. "She was not and never [was] a washer-woman, nor ever, a finicky word, laundress, so much as she was a high priestess of cleanliness. She washed and sunned and wind-swept and ironed whatever needed it, for herself and the town, which was her home, because that was the port of what she could do that her home and her town needed, and with[out] this talent of hers would be to that extent bereft—." It may be the sight of this lady washing that provided the descriptive portrait for Mrs. Spencer's poem "Lady, Lady," a poem less about a "washer-woman" than about "a high priestess of cleanliness":

> Lady, Lady, I saw your hands,
> Twisted, awry, like crumpled roots,
> Bleached poor white in a sudsy tub,
> Wrinkled and drawn from your rub-a-dub.
> Lady, Lady, I saw your heart,
> And altared there in its darksome place
> Were the tongues of flame the ancients knew,
> Where the good God sits to spangle through.

It is also possible that the poem is based on Cousin Lou, a lady who lived on Pierce Street and who was well known and well liked in the community. In her Notebooks Mrs. Spencer recorded several fond memories about Cousin Lou, and in her many oral comments about her it is evident that Mrs. Spencer held a deep fondness and respect for the lady. Her attitude toward Cousin Lou and the lady who did the family's laundry was basically the same, so much so that without a specific reference to the name Cousin Lou, one cannot distinguish between the numerous entries in her Notebooks about these two ladies.

When Sarah Louise came to live with the Spencers in the early 1920s, she took over most of the duties of running the house. An excellent cook by profession and choice, she did most of the family's cooking and, being the domineering person she was, practically ran the house after Annie went to work at Dunbar High School.

So before she went to Dunbar High School as librarian, Annie Spencer had what her son described as an easy life. Her routine would be to sleep until eleven, bathe until noon, and sit before the window and brush her hair until about two, when she would dress and come downstairs about three in the afternoon. She would spend the rest of the day in her garden working with the plants or in the garden house writing and reading. Sometimes she would join the family for dinner, but more often (especially after she went to work) she would take her dinner tray to the garden house and remain there until dark. In the evenings she would spend time with the family. But when the entire household was asleep, she could be found reading and writing until two or three in the morning. Her daughter-in-law Anne—"my daughter by law and by spirit," Mrs. Spencer often said—remembers that after Mrs. Spencer left her library job in 1946, her daily routine was little altered from that described by Chauncey. More than once Mrs. Spencer said that she would compose lines for her poems while sitting by the window brushing her hair for an hour or more. In the evenings when she retired to the garden house, she expanded many of these lines into ordered verse.

4 🦋 Publishing Career

About 1917–1918 several blacks in Lynchburg began to organize committees in order to help their race socially, economically, and legally. Annie Spencer and several other people belonged to a human relations committee which, in its desire for more positive and more immediate results in alleviating the racial tension in Lynchburg, proposed affiliation with the National Association for the Advancement of Colored People by establishing a local chapter in Lynchburg. The NAACP agreed to send an official from its main office to Lynchburg to help the members of the committee organize a local chapter, but there was the problem of housing him—for at that time there were few if any public facilities where blacks could stay in Lynchburg. So the committee, as it had done on other occasions when public figures visited the community in some public capacity, sought to have a family in the community house this representative. But for some reason, Mrs. Spencer said, no one wanted the responsibility at this time, and finally the Spencers agreed to house the guest.

Just before the person was to arrive, Edward contracted his "third spell of pneumonia." Concerned that a visitor in the house might cause Edward some discomfort, she asked to be relieved of this obligation. "I went [upstairs] to the room looking after Pop. He said, 'Mother, when does this Mr. Johnson arrive'? I said, 'I'm not going to take him and you're just getting over the pneumonia. I told him I couldn't.' He said, 'Don't tell him that. Besides, it's our only chance to see and meet people, living here in Lynchburg. Take it. He may make it more cheerful.'" So Annie gave in. Edward said that having such a noted person in the house would be good for the family, especially for the children. However, they had no clear idea at that time exactly who this Mr. Johnson was, only that he was an official of the NAACP and therefore important.

Born in Jacksonville, Florida, in 1871, James Weldon Johnson completed his early schooling there, later attending the preparatory and then the collegiate division of Atlanta University, from which he received an undergraduate degree in 1894. Returning to Jacksonville, he first worked as a teacher and then principal in the Stanton school. Among other varied activities, he organized a newspaper, studied law, and passed the Florida bar examination. By the turn of the century his interests carried him to the Broadway theatrical district where, with his brother Rosamond, he worked as a song writer. His political interests and activities gained him an appointment as a United States consul in Puerto Cabello, Venezuela (1906 to 1909) and in Nicaragua (1909 to 1912). In 1912 he published anonymously his only novel, *The Autobiography of an Ex-Coloured Man*. In 1917 he published his first volume of poetry, *Fifty Years and Other Poems*. Having joined the NAACP in 1916 as field secretary, in 1918 and 1919, the time he first met the Spencers, he was busy traveling around the country investigating lynchings and organizing chapters of the NAACP.

During this visit Johnson and the Spencers became immediate friends and afterwards he was a frequent guest at the Spencer house on Pierce Street. He enjoyed the company of Annie and Edward, and was somewhat taken aback with Annie. "From the first, Jim and I were Jim and Anne to each other," Mrs. Spencer said. "He told a terrible tale (which I won't record) after his arrival," Mrs. Spencer recalled. Later that evening the Spencers gave a small party for him "with a whole bottle of Four Roses on the table." During the party Annie tried to get Johnson to repeat the tale to the group gathered there, but evidently he did not. Before he left Johnson did tell the family different tales about Florida.

Johnson's first visit to 1313 Pierce Street was one of the most significant events in Mrs. Spencer's life. It was the beginning of what became a delightful tradition with the Spencers of entertaining as house guests many noted persons whom they met as a result of knowing Johnson. The most fruitful result of Johnson's visit was that the poet Anne Spencer was introduced to the reading public, for it was during this visit, apparently, that Johnson "discovered" her. In the autobiographical sketch Mrs. Spencer wrote for her children in 1959, she succinctly characterized her first acquaintance with James Weldon Johnson and what this meant to her over the years: "James Weldon Johnson, by an act of God, coming my way, sent a piece to Mr. Mencken. Mencken said it's OK to print." The reference here is to her first published poem, "Before the Feast at Shushan" (published in the *Crisis* for February, 1920), which began her career as a published poet.

"I had been writing before I met James Weldon Johnson," Mrs. Spencer remarked, "always jotting down things here and there." Sometimes she would awake in the middle of the night and write down something, somewhere—a "habit" she never was able to break. Even some of the books in her library have their blank pages filled with lines of poetry, critical evaluations of or responses to ideas in the books, or "just thoughts." She remarked that she always had written primarily for her own enjoyment and not for publication or praise. During his first visit Johnson saw some of her poems lying around the house and asked to take copies of them with him. "He showed them to H. L. Mencken, who said, 'Tell that woman to put beginnings and ends to her poems; I can't make heads or tails of them—but they're good,'" she recalled. She took Mencken's advice in this case, "and that's how 'Before the Feast of Shushan' got a title."

Though Mencken seems to have praised the poetic promise in the poem, it appears, however, that he was not completely pleased with the manuscript of "Before the Feast of Shushan" (Mrs. Spencer in 1972 substituted "at" for "of" in the title) as it was presented to him, and thus wrote her a somewhat "cold" commentary. In 1919 in a letter to her, Johnson wrote:

. . . glad you took Mr. Mencken's criticism like a good fellow. So many beginners are unable to take frank criticism unless that criticism is praise.

I wish you would work the poem over. I hope, also, that you will send some shorter things that I may forward to Mr. Mencken.[1]

"Jim," Mrs. Spencer said, "was almost pleading with me to shorten 'Shushan'; not because it affected him or me, but because one had to be elated with what Mencken said or he wouldn't be bothered with you." True to her nature, she apparently did not give in to Mencken's criticism in this case, which may account for "Before the Feast at Shushan" being first published in the *Crisis*, instead of in a journal or magazine edited by Mencken. She seldom spoke about such incidents as this, but one surmises from what little she said and implied that she encountered problems that many black writers whom she knew faced during the 1920s; black writers publishing during the period of the Harlem Renaissance were not as independent as one might think, and had to rely many times on what influential white editors wanted to see published. In many ways, the Harlem Renaissance was almost as white as it was black. Langston Hughes, though writing about a different aspect of this situation, captured the spirit of the more independent black artists of the 1920s (to which Mrs. Spencer belongs in spirit though not in subject matter) when he wrote in 1926 that:

We younger Negro artists who create now intend to express our individual dark-skinned selves without fear or shame. If white people are pleased we are glad. If they are not, it doesn't matter. We know we are beautiful. And ugly too. The tom-tom cries and the tom-tom laughs. If colored people are pleased we are glad. If they are not, their displeasure doesn't matter either. We build our temples for tomorrow, strong as we

---

1. James Weldon Johnson to Anne Spencer, April 16, 1919. Unless otherwise indicated, all letters between James Weldon Johnson and Anne Spencer cited in this book are located in the James Weldon Johnson Memorial Collection of Negro Arts and Letters, Collection of American Literature, Beinecke Rare Book and Manuscript Library, Yale University. Printed here by permission of Mrs. James Weldon Johnson and Yale University Library.

know how, and we stand on top of the mountain, free within our-selves.[2]

Though about the same time Mrs. Spencer wrote that she dis-agreed with "the Tom-Tom *forced* into poetry," she certainly shared Hughes's declaration of the artist's independence of ex-pression.

She may or may not have reworked "Before the Feast at Shus-han" before returning it to James Weldon Johnson for publica-tion in the *Crisis*. However, prior to its printing, Johnson de-cided to do some editing which seems to have irritated the new poet. Having changed the title, he wrote to ask: "Had the title The Feast of Shushan ever struck you as one for the poem?"[3] Mrs. Spencer replied:

I do not like the title "The Feast of Shushan." How can you see it so? I used "Before the Feast" as being interpretive. Many times the King and Queen must have been together in the beautiful garden; this particular time Vashti *tried* to tell the old beast what love really meant—in the last two verses I have had the King repeat in reflective monologue (without quotation marks) something of the 'new thing' that she aimed to teach him. You see, the Feast had never taken place. That Ahasuerus re-mained unchanged by his lesson we know from the tragic outcome of the feast, an episode happening later, as recorded in Esther.

If you don't do *that* [change the title back to its original], I promise not to bombard you with letters much longer.[4]

After such a determined statement from her, Johnson replied: "I won't change the title of your poem. Of course, I see that you are right."[5]

Mrs. Spencer said that she wrote "At the Carnival" (and sev-eral other poems) long before she wrote "Shushan," but this was

2. Langston Hughes, "The Negro Artist and the Racial Mountain," *Nation*, June 23, 1926, pp. 692–94. The article was written in response to George S. Schuyler, "The Negro-Art Hokum," *Nation*, June 16, 1926, pp. 662–63.

3. James Weldon Johnson to Anne Spencer, undated (September 14 pen-ciled in, probably by Anne Spencer).

4. Anne Spencer to James Weldon Johnson, January 1, 1920.

5. James Weldon Johnson to Anne Spencer, January 8, 1920. Though a penciled note on the back of this letter refers to the poem as "Translation," it is obvious that "Before the Feast at Shushan" is the poem in question.

Annie Bethal Scales, age fourteen

Annie Scales Spencer, age twenty-three

Anne and Edward Spencer in their garden (1937)

Anne Spencer House and Garden Historic Landmark

The little garden house "Edankraal"

Anne Spencer, age eighty-nine (1971)

her first published poem. And Johnson, initiating her coming-out, decided on a "pen name" and informed her of it: "I have decided that Anne Spencer is the way in which you should sign—that makes a splendid pen name." [6] Annie Scales Spencer agreed: "I like the pen name—really I like every thing that belongs to me!" [7] Since that time, as citizen and poet she was known outside her immediate family primarily as Anne Spencer.

In 1922 James Weldon Johnson edited *The Book of American Negro Poetry* and included five poems by Anne Spencer. The book went to press in November, 1921, and Johnson wrote to her at the beginning of the month for a short biographical sketch. On the back of the letter requesting this information, Anne Spencer, probably in 1942, wrote in pencil: "Sorry, *this* was a tentative biog. sketch. Tried a lot of 'em to see which tale sounded best." [8]

Johnson made an error in his book when he stated that Anne Spencer was born in Bramwell, West Virginia. Either shortly before or shortly after the book was published, "Pop looked at what Mr. Johnson had written and said, 'Mother, this is wrong. Mr. Johnson says that you were born in Bramwell, but we told him that is where we were married.'" Mr. Spencer went on to say that they should write Johnson right away and ask that he make the correction. Johnson "was upset in telling me 'I'll write and change it'; but I said no, let it stay. I am happy to have been born in a free state." Since then editors have recorded her birthplace as Bramwell.

Among the many reviews of Johnson's *The Book of American Negro Poetry* was that of Walter White in the *Liberator* (April, 1922). (Walter White [1893–1955] was an ardent fighter for the civil rights of American blacks. For many years he was executive secretary of the NAACP, and has been praised for his probing investigations into lynchings in the United States. Novelist, es-

6. James Weldon Johnson to Anne Spencer, undated (September 14, 1921, penciled in).
7. Anne Spencer to James Weldon Johnson, January 1, 1920.
8. James Weldon Johnson to Anne Spencer, November 2, 1921.

sayist, biographer, and statesman, between 1925 and 1955 he was an adviser to various governmental officials and agencies.) White devoted half of his review to Anne Spencer and "Before the Feast at Shushan": "Upon what sort of poetry does Mr. Johnson base his assertion of hopes of poetic achievement by the Negro? Here is a fragment of a poem by Anne Spencer, a woman whose work deserves far greater notice than it is receiving." Johnson informed Anne Spencer of the review and sent her a copy of it. She promptly replied: "Interested! I was thoroughly thrilled by my first review. I can scarcely wait for my copy of the real book which Bethel is sending on to me. And too, I had not seen a copy of the 'Liberator' before." [9] Other reviews of the anthology called attention to Anne Spencer's talent and poetic promise. In the *Nation* (June 7, 1922) Walter White wrote: "Had Mr. Johnson done nothing else than introduce us to the work of Anne Spencer in her charming Before the Feast of Shushan and her beautiful The Wife-Woman, or to the vigor and genuine merit of Claude McKay, he would have done well." In the *New Republic* (July 12, 1922) Robert Littell remarked that "Miss Spencer has great mastery over dreamy, half-mystical melodies."

Inclusion in Johnson's anthology brought Anne Spencer immediate attention as a competent poet. But even before a number of black editors and anthologists began to seek manuscripts for publication from her, Robert T. Kerlin (1886–1950), literary critic and a professor of English and history at various schools and colleges in the eastern United States, noticed her sparse publications and asked for new poems to include in his proposed anthology of black writers, *Negro Poets and Their Poems* (1923). For this publication she sent him one of her now most popular poems, "At the Carnival." Kerlin responded: "Just to thank you, thank you so much, for your kindness in sending me a copy of the ever admirable poem, *At the Carnival*. I like it extremely on repeated readings. Its philosophy (implied), its way

9. Anne Spencer to James Weldon Johnson, April 12, 1922.

of looking at life and people, is altogether sound. Therefore we —my wife and I—think you a wonderful woman, a rare and select being. Without seeing you we love you. And from our hearts, from the very depths of them, we wish and pray for your happiness."[10] Kerlin, Mrs. Spencer said, was mocked for doing such an anthology, and, partly as a result of this but mainly as a result of his other "humanitarian" activities associated with blacks—publishing several articles and pamphlets on the subject of racial discrimination—he lost his job at Virginia Military Institute after ten years of service there. He left and assumed a teaching position at State Normal School in West Chester, Pennsylvania. Reviewing *Negro Poets and Their Poems* for the *New Republic* (June 4, 1924), Eric D. Walrond, calling Kerlin "a martyr to the cause of Negro liberty," added that "in 1919, while on the faculty of Virginia Military Institute, he wrote a letter to the Governor of Arkansas in which he pleaded for the release of the Elaine rioters, and was forthwith dismissed from the Institute." In her autobiographical sketch Anne Spencer, in 1959, recalled the event: "Robert T. Kerlin . . . came in from Lexington to see us. Shortly afterward he lost his faculty post for writing protest articles defending humanity—if brown. How long it seems and how rocky!"

When James Weldon Johnson had asked Anne Spencer to send him her poems so that he could pass them on to H. L. Mencken, he was busy traveling throughout the country as a representative for the NAACP, and Anne Spencer, probably eager as any newly published writer to have immediate evaluation of her poems, wanted to send them directly to Mencken and avoid the intermediary. She got Johnson's approval to do this, but it seems that, contrary to Johnson's assumptions, she did not take Mencken's "frank criticism" like a "good fellow." She maintained that Mencken was hard on her poetry, that he was not a poet and thus was not receptive to some of the things she was trying to do in her poems.

10. Robert T. Kerlin to Anne Spencer, April 23, [1922], in Spencer Family Papers.

In addition to bringing Anne Spencer's poetry to the attention of Mencken and other critics and arranging for it to be published, Johnson tried to help the young poet improve her writing. He often sent her books dealing with the writing of poetry as well as newly published anthologies of contemporary poetry. He believed that though her poetry showed a remarkable talent, it was a little "too unconventional" in experimenting with the "newer forms" gaining impetus in the 1920s. In early 1920 he sent her a copy of Marguerite Wilkinson's *New Voices*, explaining that it "deals with the *newer forms* of poetry, and those are the forms which are your natural means of expression." [11] He also suggested that a reading of Edna St. Vincent Millay's "Renascence" would be valuable to her. Later, in 1931, he wrote her to "get a copy of 'The Poems of Gerard Manley Hopkins'—Oxford Press. I shall be greatly mistaken if you do not find closer kinship with him than with any poet you know." [12] After some difficulty, Anne Spencer located a copy of Hopkins's poems. Having read them, she wrote to Johnson: "If ever exposed to Holy rollerism I'd be a High Priestess—and this time being thoroly enamored of I, myself and me, here is formed the odious triumvirate, Browning—Hopkins—me. Tho I never heard the middle poet's name till you called it." [13]

After recognizing inherent talent in Anne Spencer's early poetry, both Mencken and Johnson suggested she write prose. And early in her career Anne Spencer did write prose, but she said in later years that she never published any. Writing to Johnson in 1922, she alluded to Mencken's suggestion (and probably referred to some of her prose he rejected two years earlier): "My mind swears to make him accept prose from me—whenever there is time to write it." [14] Later she informed Johnson of a story on which she was working. He answered:

I am glad to know you are working on your story. You are right keep-

11. James Weldon Johnson to Anne Spencer, January 9, [1920?].
12. James Weldon Johnson to Anne Spencer, February 5 (1931 penciled in).
13. Anne Spencer to James Weldon Johnson, March 22, 1931.
14. Anne Spencer to James Weldon Johnson, April 12, 1922.

ing the propaganda out, unless it is so disguised as not to be discovered, except by the most skilled eye. . . . This is the great moment for literature on the race question. You ought to set for yourself the task of doing your story and having it ready to submit to a publisher for spring publication. When it comes to getting a publisher, you know you can depend on me for all I may be able to do; and besides, you already have the great Mencken interested in your work.[15]

She completed an article and story—but probably not within the year as Johnson had suggested—both of which seem to have been rejected for publication. In two letters to Johnson she spoke of them. Since the dates for both letters are uncertain, it is difficult to determine if she spoke of the same story in both letters. In the first letter she wrote: "I do, though, have an article for Mencken, and a story I want you and Mr. White to see. Mr. White is to read the story last—he promised."[16] The article may have been one titled "Madame and Maid" that Johnson mentioned in a letter to her: "Let me say that you must, by all means, do the article 'Madame and Maid.' I feel sure that you can get it accepted by the *New Republic*, the *Dial* or some such publication, if it is well done; and I feel especially sure that you can do it well. If I were near you I'd actually make you do these things."[17] If this is indeed the article in question, Anne Spencer finished it and sent it to Johnson, who tried to get it published. In 1920 he wrote informing her that the article, apparently a political one, had been rejected for publication.[18] Perhaps it was Mencken who rejected the article (and who may have rejected others of hers), and her statement in 1922 that "my mind swears to make him accept prose from me" could refer to Mencken's rejection of this particular article of "political" prose. This incident may have discouraged Mrs. Spencer from submitting other such articles for publication. She often remarked that she had submitted only one poem for publication; it was rejected and she never sub-

15. James Weldon Johnson to Anne Spencer, September 2 (1924 penciled in).
16. Anne Spencer to James Weldon Johnson, Sunday, undated.
17. James Weldon Johnson to Anne Spencer, March [19, 1919?].
18. James Weldon Johnson to Anne Spencer, November 30, 1920. See also the annotation on the back of this letter.

mitted another of her own. If indeed discouraged by Mencken's criticism of her political prose, she did share many of his views, especially those about the South. It just might be that she was speaking of this same article when she asked Johnson (in yet a third undated letter): "Did you read Mencken's Sterilization article [perhaps "The Sahara of the Bozart"]—it was my own dictum without his clever sapience, some months before." [19]

The prose in question could have been a story or an article titled "White Man," which also seems to have been rejected. She alluded to this title in the second undated letter: "Dreadfully sorry that 'White Man' came to nothing—I almost did too—I am writing Mr. White to please do it since he likes the idea. My muses are all dead—even a muse—quite sure the younger ones must do the 'carrying on.'" [20]

In spite of continued urgings from Mencken, Johnson, and others that she devote time to writing prose, there is no evidence at this time that Anne Spencer ever submitted for publication any literary prose except a review of Johnson's autobiography *Along This Way* in a teachers' journal (to which she alluded in a letter to him) and a review of Georgia Douglas Johnson's book of poems, *Autumn Love Cycle* (1928), for the *Crisis* (March, 1929). She did, however, in another letter (probably to Johnson) mention what seems to be another article: "I've got some ruminations of my own about an alliterative subject, Popes and Prostitutes. They made us what we think we are today. True, Frazer's Golden Bough is the accepted unit on Religion and [sees?] through the ages. He demonstrates Identity; I but show how this oneness operated to bring the new deal to our wishful ego. All our contrivances for comfort date back to the Vestal Virgins and the Augurs: Cushions, beds, forks, silken adornments, and washing machines." [21]

After the early 1920s, her literary life involved whites as well

---

19. Anne Spencer to James Weldon Johnson, undated.
20. Anne Spencer to James Weldon Johnson, Saturday, undated. The reference here could be to her poem titled "White Things."
21. Anne Spencer to [James Weldon Johnson], Saturday, midnight, undated.

as blacks who were writers or who were interested in literature. In two letters to Johnson (internal evidence dates them about 1934) she mentioned what evidently was her early contact with Murrell Edmunds (poet, novelist, dramatist) and his brother Abe, two whites in Lynchburg who apparently came to know Anne Spencer as a direct result of her publications. In the first of these letters to Johnson she made what appears to be a reference to the Edmunds brothers: "Young white fellow poet gave several copies of his and brother's poems; nice F. F. V. family last word . . . [he] *has* written a book and wants you to review it—somewhere. Came lugging up the hill to my work-place the other day with a book for each of us, and made me swear I'd send yours on and beg your help." [22] In the second of these two letters she wrote Johnson again concerning, among other things, Edmunds's manuscript: "Days before your cruel Lynchville [probably an article on lynchings in the South] arrived, a local pastor had been to borrow the biography of James Wilson Johnson. . . . It was like this. He is a darling, and as helpless as the Swanee River Negro often is, and so credulous; these darling nordics are infants by comparison—Now—one of these, Murrell Edmunds, brother of Abe . . . comes to me in the midst of my grubby job, to ask the Boon of sending his book ms. to you. . . . It's Negro stuff, of course." [23] What began as a literary association between Mrs. Spencer and Edmunds developed into a lifelong friendship. The same can be said for other persons (black and white) in Lynchburg interested in literature who came to know Anne Spencer after she became a published poet.

At least once after becoming a published poet, Anne Spencer decided to write a novel, and probably wrote at least part of it. She alluded to such a novel more than once in her letters to Johnson. For instance: "Thanks for the clipping reminder. The prize book is to be a quiet, sympathetic satire on the social life of the Negro *here* on Main Street. Yclept 'The Best People.' Can

22. Anne Spencer to [James Weldon Johnson], November 7, undated.
23. Anne Spencer to James Weldon Johnson, November 9, undated.

you see my darling sister-in-law therein?"[24] Perhaps Anne
Spencer not only wrote at least part of her satirical novel about
the residents on "Main Street," but also made these residents
aware of her satire. If this was the case, it might explain a somewhat confusing statement in an undated letter to Johnson: "I
daren't show my freckles on our Main Street." In 1934 she wrote:
"I owe *you* one American novel and intend to pay within the
year—or forever shut up . . . so encouraged do I feel."[25] Still
trying to encourage her to write prose, Johnson promptly responded: "No, I have not forgotten that you are the author of a
still born novel; but you really must do something about that.
You can write it and you know you can write it and you ought to
do it. If you do not do it within a year, I shall be left with no re-
course but to recommend that you be led out some morning and
shot at sunrise."[26]

It appears that the novel was not forthcoming within the year,
and Anne Spencer, true to her word, did not speak of working
on it again in her letters to Johnson, so far as the available letters
show. In later years she said, seemingly in earnest, that she actually never wrote the novel, but that she "planned one about a
white man who passes for colored" and would mention working on it to keep Johnson and other friends from pressing her.
There is no doubt in my mind that she actually did write parts of
it, if not the entire novel. Among her papers there are scattered
pages of prose fiction which easily could belong to this projected
novel. In addition, Murrell Edmunds in a letter to me (July 13,
1972) provided an unsolicited comment on a novel Anne Spencer was working on at one time:

On occasion I would send or carry her some of my work, and she always had wise and gentle comments to make about it. And she, on her
part, on one of my visits to the [Dunbar] High School Library, read me
the opening pages of a projected novel she was writing. I do not know if
she ever finished it, but I remember to this day—against a background

24. Anne Spencer to James Weldon Johnson, Saturday, undated.
25. Anne Spencer to James Weldon Johnson, May 7, 1934.
26. James Weldon Johnson to Anne Spencer, May 10, 1934.

of black school children at study, warily watching the presence of a white man in their midst—those clear rounded sentences and the sound of her deep, muted voice and the kind of imagery with which only a born poet manages to enrich prose.

Johnson introduced the poet through the magazine with which he was personally associated, the *Crisis*, and through his 1922 anthology of black poets. The following year, 1923, Robert T. Kerlin included her in his *Negro Poets and Their Poems*, and Louis Untermeyer included Anne Spencer and one other black American poet, Claude McKay, in his *American Poetry Since 1900*. She was not altogether pleased with this: "He put us in the Jim Crow section—but I wrote and thanked him for the inclusion." She said that she should not have felt offended by being included in the "Jim Crow section," that Untermeyer was trying to do something positive.

Though when I knew her Mrs. Spencer said that she always had written poetry for reasons other than publication or praise, it appears that the yearning for approval and success which accompanies many writers' first publications (especially successful publications) affected Anne Spencer. In 1924, after becoming published and anthologized, she wrote Johnson a letter in which she voiced concern over being excluded from an anthology of black poets published that year. The bulk of the letter concerns a story Johnson had published in the *Dial* ("In a Thicket"), which Anne Spencer analyzed at his request, though she was unaware at the time that Johnson had written it. The analysis of the story (which is among the Spencer papers in the Johnson Collection at Yale) contains interesting commentary on literature and literary criticism by and about black people of the time. In conjunction with her comment in the letter on the story, she ended with: "It's just for crimes like the above that the 'Durham People of Importance' kept me out of their Anthology. Served me right, you say?" [27] In the same letter Mrs. Spencer

27. Anne Spencer to James Weldon Johnson, June 23, 1924. The reference is probably to Newman I. White and W. C. Jackson (eds.), *An Anthology of Verse by American Negroes* (Durham, N.C.: Trinity College Press, 1924).

spoke of a particularly despondent time in her life: "All my stars surely combine to make me immensely unhappy." It may not be erroneous to read this remark as having some connection with her concern over being excluded from the anthology.

The generally despondent tone of the letter probably prompted Johnson to write a conciliatory note concerning the anthology:

> That was a first class analysis of the *Dial* story.
>
> As I read your letter through I became more and more convinced that Mencken is right. You ought to devote yourself to writing prose. You have a prose style that few of us possess. You had better get to work on those stories.
>
> I do not think you lost very much by being kept out of the Durham anthology, and you must remember that you are in the greatest anthology on earth.[28]

Aware of her capabilities, she was also aware of her limitations as a poet. She accepted, though probably somewhat despondently, Mencken's initial criticism of her poetry. No doubt crestfallen when her article and story were rejected for publication, she was appreciative of Johnson's evaluations of her writings and his attempts to help her improve her art. About two years or so after Johnson showed her works to Mencken, he wrote her for new poems to include in some proposed publication venture with Claude McKay. She responded: "I shall love writing with Mr. McKay immensely. Tho I have no poems now save the one of 'MacSwiney' which I renamed 'Resurgence' [now left untitled]. You see, Mr. Mencken dissuaded me. I took him quite to heart; a refractory heart, I confess, that still yearns toward numbers."[29]

In turn, Johnson often asked Anne Spencer's opinions of his own writings, sometimes without letting her know that the work to be appraised was his own, as in the case of her review of "In a Thicket." After writing a personal review of his *God's Trombones*, she enclosed in her letter a "new sonnet" (which is ex-

---

28. James Weldon Johnson to Anne Spencer, July 10, 1924.
29. Anne Spencer to James Weldon Johnson, April 12, 1922.

cluded from her available manuscript materials) and remarked: "I'm so partial to my things it mayn't be good."[30]

The 1920 publication of "Before the Feast at Shushan" attracted the attention of many figures associated with the Harlem movement, which was to reach its peak in the middle of the decade. Editors of magazines (such as Charles S. Johnson of *Opportunity*), persons indirectly associated with magazines (such as Walter White for the *Crisis*), and writers editing special "Negro issues" for various magazines (Alain Locke for *Survey Graphic*, Countee Cullen for *Palms*, Lewis Alexander for *Carolina Magazine*) as well as anthologists (such as Cullen and Alain Locke) wrote Anne Spencer throughout the 1920s asking for manuscripts to publish. Sometimes she obliged them and sometimes she did not. Adding to its earlier publications of her poems, the *Crisis* published "White Things" (March, 1923), and "Grapes: Still-Life" (April, 1929); *Survey Graphic* published "Lady, Lady" (March, 1925); *Palms* published "Lines to a Nasturtium" (October, 1926); *Opportunity* published "Rime for the Christmas Baby" (December, 1927).

Anne Spencer was among the black writers included in *The New Negro* (1925), edited by Alain Locke, which was one of the most important publications to come out of the Harlem Renaissance as well as one of the most significant interpretative publications in black American literary history. In 1927 appeared Countee Cullen's anthology of black poetry, *Caroling Dusk*; in it he included ten poems by Anne Spencer, the largest selection of her poetry ever to appear in a single volume. Reviewing the anthology in the Holiday of Books section of the *Detroit Free Press* (November 27, 1927), Amey Smyth stated that "Anne Spencer, of Lynchburg, Virginia, who wields the cold pen of a Negro Amy Lowell," was one of the outstanding contributors to this volume.

In all, less than thirty of Anne Spencer's poems have been published. Beginning in 1920, her career as a published poet

30. Anne Spencer to James Weldon Johnson, December 30, undated.

lasted a little over ten years. The last original poem by her to appear in a periodical publication was "Requiem," which appeared in the *Lyric* (Spring, 1931). But the poems of hers known to have been published have been widely anthologized, appearing in almost every major anthology of black American poetry in the 1920s, 1930s, and 1940s. Critical histories and general American literature anthologies which cover black American writers during the period in which her poems were published usually include some comment on her poetry.

In addition to being included in various anthologies of black American writing between 1920 and 1950 (and after), Anne Spencer's poetry appeared in at least one college textbook which was not black oriented. In 1934 she was asked permission to include two of her poems, "At the Carnival" and "Questing," in the third and revised edition of *Fundamentals of Speech: A Textbook of Delivery*, "prepared by Professor Joseph Smith, of the University of Utah." The letter pointed out that the book, "by the way, is not an anthology." [31] Flattered over the request, she informed Johnson of her new achievement, and commented on the latter poem: "*Questing* is an 'ookey piece—praps using to point out, D-O-N-T! Anyway, I'm tickled." [32] This inclusion was in fact an unusual event. Few texts of this sort until recent times included any poems by black American poets, and those that did usually chose James Weldon Johnson's "The Creation" or some poem written in dialect or one that was unquestionably about blacks.

Many people who have known her as a poet have often characterized Anne Spencer as shy when it concerned her writings. Though not courting public notice for her poems, she did welcome personal appraisal from her friends, and many times she included poems in letters to them. She once sent a group of poems to W. E. B. Du Bois, who proposed entering them in a

31. Harriet E. Robinson (for Harper & Bros.) to Anne Spencer, April 18, 1934, in the James Weldon Johnson Memorial Collection of Negro Arts and Letters.
32. Anne Spencer to James Weldon Johnson, May 7, 1934.

writing contest (probably one held by *Opportunity*). She shied away from the proposal and cautioned Johnson to help prevent this exposure: "The poems were not sent to Mr. Du Bois to be entered in contest—told him *not*; and if any one of them gains the vice presidency of honorable mention, I'll sue him for breach of promise." [33]

Many new poets, after their first publications or after receiving praise for such publications, usually submit—and often have published—a large number of poems of questionable merit; such was not the case with Anne Spencer. She was not only "partial" to her "things," but also concerned with perfection and self-evaluation. She would not allow her literary friends to submit for publication any of her poems with which she was not completely satisfied (though others pointed out valid shortcomings in the poems after she had allowed them to be published). This in part accounts for her sparse publication record. Moreover, she was so busy working in her garden and "taking care of her family" that there was often no time for writing and perfecting. Many friends urged her to write and to publish. She recalled that Langston Hughes wrote a line in the *Crisis* about her limited productions: "There is an unsharpened pencil on Anne Spencer's table."

But the appeals from her friends did not break her literary silence. Until the end of his life, James Weldon Johnson constantly urged her to write and to publish more; he never gave up his appeals that she devote time to prose publications: "Every time I get a good letter from you—and they are consistently good—I enjoy it so much that it makes me mad. Mad because, despite the fact that you write finer, sharper, more brilliant prose than almost anybody I know, I cannot, with all my entreating, cajoling or browbeating, get you to write the story that you could write so well. I know of nothing left to do but to actually beat you." [34]

33. Anne Spencer to James Weldon Johnson, Saturday, undated.
34. James Weldon Johnson to Anne Spencer, November 1 (1937 penciled in).

That her desire to see her "private thoughts" given public exposure declined after 1930 can be seen in her letters to Carl Van Vechten. When in the early 1940s Van Vechten began assembling the James Weldon Johnson Memorial Collection of Negro Arts and Letters at Yale University, he asked Mrs. Spencer for her letters to Johnson to include in the collection, as well as for her own manuscripts. She replied: "I wouldn't wish my letters, if any, to go in the collection unless I edited them: I'm afraid . . . surely, that in those days I was ingenuous enough to try to appear intellectual without being intelligent."[35] And the letters which she edited and submitted to the collection, to be sure, were not a majority of the ones she possessed at that time. Van Vechten, closely associated with many figures who gained prominence during and after the Harlem Renaissance period, was aware of Mrs. Spencer's reluctance to publish and of her friends' desire that she do so. Writing to her about the collection, he brought up the subject of her writing prose. Her response: "I'll never do the book nor the story now, but at 60-odd I still have a colossal reserve of constructive indignation. I'd like to do a column some where headed 'Roses named after Them.'"[36]

35. Anne Spencer to Carl Van Vechten, June 24, 1943, in the Carl Van Vechten Collection, Collection of American Literature, Beinecke Rare Book and Manuscript Library, Yale University.

36. Anne Spencer to Carl Van Vechten, undated (the envelope is postmarked June 16, 1943), *ibid*.

5 ✠ Literary Acquaintances

Little did Edward Spencer know in 1917–1918 when he urged his wife to house the NAACP official (James Weldon Johnson) how much this would eventually allow the family access to avenues outside the spiritually deadening existence in Lynchburg, and that such a contact would prove even more important for Anne. Mrs. Spencer characterized her initial meeting with Johnson as "an act of God." To be sure, her life between 1920 and 1940 was spiritually stimulated as a direct consequence of her friendship with Johnson.

The Spencers—especially Edward—loved to entertain. Johnson's visits and the friends whom he introduced to the Spencers increased their opportunities to entertain, for many of these new-found friends became guests at 1313 Pierce Street and in return invited Edward and Anne to New York, Washington, D.C., Atlanta, and other places, where their social and intellectual contacts were widened.

During the first half of this century Lynchburg was a strategic stopover point between Washington and points north, and Nashville, Atlanta, and other points south. The people whom the Spencers came to know after about 1920 frequently used their home as a resting and intellectually stimulating place to stop when traveling. It is common knowledge that at that time traveling blacks often were hard pressed for stopover areas since public accommodations for them were rare. Lynchburg became an oasis in a desert of public racial discrimination. Leaving Washington in the morning (where public accommodations could be found fairly easily, though many were segregated) a black could travel to Lynchburg by car or train and arrive in the evening. There he or she could have a leisurely rest and leave early in the morning and arrive in time to find other accommodations in another fairly large southern town. But the Spencers' guests did not use 1313 Pierce Street only as a convenient half-way house; often they deliberately took this route in order to visit the Spencers, and many times 1313 Pierce was their final destination.

When their out-of-town guests would arrive, the Spencers would go all out to make them comfortable. At times Edward would rent a car (before he bought his own) and give them a guided tour of the area. The Spencers often would give parties and small receptions for noted guests. Such occasions allowed many of Lynchburg's black (and white) citizens to meet people who otherwise would not ordinarily have come to Lynchburg. 1313 Pierce Street got a reputation within the black community for being a nice and comfortable place for "important" people to stay; it acquired the same reputation within black society on the Eastern seaboard. On many occasions the seminary would ask the Spencers to house the school's guests, since the school itself could not comfortably accommodate them and they were barred from public facilities. 1313 Pierce Street became so popular that it was only a few years after 1920 that people in the public eye were meeting one another through the Spencers.

Even white citizens of Lynchburg were aware of the popularity of 1313 Pierce Street. One white citizen who remembers clearly the 1930s and 1940s remarked to me that if important people came to town—black or white—they often could be found as guests at 1313 Pierce, and that several whites in Lynchburg courted introductions to "these important people" through Edward and Anne Spencer. Doctors, lawyers, singers, entertainers, college presidents, politicians, scientists, sociologists, writers, and artists were among the many guests over the years —such names as Paul Robeson, Roland Hayes, Walter White, Charles S. Johnson, George Washington Carver, Adam Clayton Powell, W. E. B. Du Bois, Langston Hughes, and Georgia Douglas Johnson.

Mrs. Spencer said that she had met only two people in her life that she "utterly despised," and both were guests in her home: one was George Washington Carver and the other was a former president of Virginia State College (Petersburg). Both men displayed an intolerable arrogance and scorned the common black person; both were despicably self-impressed. "After meeting them I could have written 'White Things,'" Mrs. Spencer said. The college president stated to her that even his wife could not see him in his office unless she had an appointment, and that he had absolutely no time for the lower levels of black society. "I asked him if ever he had thought of what he would do if the building were on fire and the janitor was the only person who knew but had not made an appointment to see him. He didn't answer. He was the most odious man who ever ate at this table," Mrs. Spencer said.

More than once the atmosphere became strained between Anne Spencer and one of her "uppity" guests, for Mrs. Spencer did not condone social and intellectual pretensions. If she and Edward were entertaining, they made no distinctions among their guests in terms of social standing, financial assets, or academic laurels. Sometimes one of the "uppity" guests would make a condescending remark about another guest's misuse of grammar or lack of knowledge of a certain subject or "crudeness" in social graces, only to have Anne Spencer "put them in their place" and reassert that 1313 Pierce Street belonged to the Spencers and *anyone* there was there by invitation and would be treated with respect.

One of the most widely known persons to visit the Spencers over the years was W. E. B. Du Bois, whom Mrs. Spencer first met in 1897. Mrs. Spencer remembered that their second meeting was in late spring, though she could not recall the exact year. Du Bois was in Lynchburg visiting Virginia Theological Seminary and College. The seminary had made provisions for him to be housed at the school during his stay but at that time the seminary was still struggling to improve its physical facilities, and Du Bois discovered, to his chagrin, that the seminary did not have proper bathing facilities for him. "Irritated," Mrs. Spencer said, is not the word to describe his reaction to this.

Edward Spencer had worked hard over the years to make his home comfortable and modern. The Spencers were one of the few black families in Lynchburg at that time to have central heating and indoor bathroom facilities (through Edward's inventive industry). Du Bois heard that the Spencers had a bath tub and asked them if he could come there to bathe. The Spencers consented. While there he exhibited a generally arrogant attitude and ridiculed the seminary for its lack of facilities—especially when such shortcomings inconvenienced the school's guests. Explaining and apologizing for his intrusion into the Spencers' private home, Du Bois said that when he asked for a bath at the seminary someone began to whisk a tin tub for his use. Anne Spencer came to the seminary's defense and explained the obvious: the lack of money to acquire modern and convenient facilities at an institution financially struggling to get teachers and supplies.

Du Bois visited the Spencers numerous times after this—and not just to use their bathtub. He and Anne had many a memorable conversation during the ensuing years. Sometimes while Du Bois was at the Spencers, he and Anne would walk in the garden, and Du Bois would talk of the many things that were on his mind: his writings, his teaching, his social work, his ideas, his disgust with American society. And Anne Spencer, with her inquisitive and alert mind, valued these conversations as an opportunity to get firsthand information about life outside Lynchburg.

The "stiffness" of the man, often interpreted as arrogance and an unyielding pride, on occasion caused heated words between him and Mrs. Spencer. On one occasion while en route to Atlanta he stopped at 1313 Pierce for a few days. Anne Spencer knew a young man from Lynchburg who was attending Atlanta University and she thought that this would be a good opportunity for him to get a ride back to school and save some money; and since Du Bois was driving the entire trip alone, she thought the young man going along would provide him company for the long trip. When she made this proposal, Du Bois inquired about the young man's background. Mrs. Spencer told him that the young man was a student at Atlanta University and came from a good Lynchburg family. Du Bois asked how "good" the family was. Praising the family highly, Mrs. Spencer added that the young man's father was a janitor. Learning this, Du Bois refused to allow this young man to ride to Atlanta with him. Anne Spencer argued that the young man's father's occupation would not taint Du Bois; that he did not even have to talk with the young man during the trip, just let him sit in the car from Lynchburg to Atlanta. Du Bois still refused, and Mrs. Spencer "gave him a good telling-off." She never forgot this and probably never forgave Du Bois for such a pompous attitude.

According to Mrs. Spencer, Du Bois' light and tender moments came, but that stiff, stern self was the dominant personality. Mrs. Spencer said that his final departure from the United States should not be misinterpreted: he migrated to Africa not because he loved the African people so much, but because he hated white America so intensely. No man like Du Bois, she maintained, would for the love of it go to a place where the general populace was poor, illiterate, and in some of the most depraved conditions imaginable. As hard as he may have tried at times, Du Bois could not interact personally and familiarly with lower-class or poor people, and could deal with them only on objective and intellectual terms. Though his personal tolerance for disadvantaged people was low, he despised the people and conditions which created such people. This man was a genius, Mrs. Spencer said, in a country which intellectually castrated his genius and which would not let him live a life for which his more than middle-class attitude yearned. Tragically, by refusing to recognize his genius, American society oppressed Du Bois as much as, if not more than, it did members of the disadvantaged masses.

That Anne Spencer held a strong intellectual attraction for Du Bois is evident from her Notebooks. In the fragments of her

Notebooks that survive, there are more entries about and addressed to Du Bois than for any of her other acquaintances. It seems plausible that one of the primary attractions Du Bois held for her was that he was of like mind: firm in his convictions, even when these convictions clashed with Anne Spencer's own. From her comments about him and their personal association, I infer that Du Bois was one who would give her an intellectually stimulating and enlightening argument, and, she said, she loved to argue. When I knew her, Anne Spencer was a woman whose grace and poise contrasted sharply with—as well as complemented—her biting and critical tongue, one who never hesitated to reject superficial social decorum and speak her mind in a dignified and self-assured manner, and in a language and attitude best suited to the occasion or topic at hand. This side of her personality, it seems to me, would have been somewhat intimidating to those who were not familiar with her and who were not of like mind. And it may be correct to assume that, as a result, many of her friends and acquaintances often let her have her way. But Du Bois would match her idea for idea, word for word. Both were unyielding and resolute in mind and manner, and perhaps this warring friendship was central in maintaining the intellectual attraction one held for the other.

Mrs. Spencer knew Claude McKay through letters and mutual friends long before she met him in New York. She remembered him as a warm and handsome man. In the 1920s she wrote him requesting an autograph in his new book that she had just bought. Her daughter, who was then living in New York, got McKay's address and went to his apartment. She knocked on the door and McKay greeted her stark naked. The young lady was embarrassed and McKay soon detected why. Calm and cool, he told her to wait outside the door and he would be with her shortly. He returned and gave her the autographed book and the two talked briefly about themselves and Mrs. Spencer.

McKay admired Anne Spencer as a person and as a poet. As a black writer, Anne Spencer had brought something fresh to the

Harlem movement, and most of the black writers welcomed her poetry. In August, 1923, Alain Locke sent her a card from Berlin: "McKay and I have met here—he was seven months in Russia —we have talked much about you, and both send you greetings."[1] When McKay returned to the United States he wrote Anne Spencer and asked her for something of hers to publish in *New Masses*. She sent him "At the Carnival," though she never had heard of *New Masses*. McKay never acknowledged receipt of the poem, and after Mrs. Spencer learned that "the magazine was associated with the Communist party," she wrote and asked that her manuscript be returned. She did not think "At the Carnival" was appropriate for such a publication. This was the weekly *New Masses* which appeared in 1926 as a revival of the *Liberator*, and not the original *New Masses*—forerunner of the *Liberator*—which was suppressed by the federal government in 1917. It is possible that she sent him a poem other than "At the Carnival," since that poem had already appeared in print.

Another of the friends of the Spencers was Sterling A. Brown, who has distinguished himself as one of the foremost black American poets, editors, and critics. One of his first jobs after graduating from college was teaching at Virginia Theological Seminary and College in Lynchburg (1923 to 1926). While living in Lynchburg he made the acquaintance of Edward and Anne Spencer. The two poets, both young in terms of publications, discussed poetry many times in the Spencer home. When Brown visited the Spencers he often would find Mrs. Spencer working in her garden and would always laugh at how dirty she got, Mrs. Spencer remembered. "He wrote a poem to me and my dirty dress," she chuckled—"To a Certain Lady, In Her Garden (For Anne Spencer)."

In more than one of Brown's poems there is evidence of his acquaintance with Anne Spencer. Mrs. Spencer often related anecdotes which support this. For example, one night when

1. Alain Locke to Anne Spencer, August, 1923, in Spencer Family Papers, Anne Spencer House and Garden Historic Landmark, Lynchburg, Virginia.

Brown was visiting the Spencer home, as he often did while living in Lynchburg, he and Edward began talking about a young black man in town who was noted for his guitar playing and songs. John "Big Boy" Davis was his name and he had a wide reputation in the area as an entertainer. "Big Boy" must have been a pleasant enough fellow, but on more than one occasion he was in jail. Brown listened to the small group gathered at 1313 Pierce Street talk about Big Boy for some time, and he lamented the fact that the musician was presently in jail and the group could not have the pleasure of his "box picking" and singing that particular night. Edward spoke up and said that this was not a problem if they really wanted to hear him. "Pop said, 'let's go down and get him out.'" Anne sat up amazed and asked, "Pop, how are you going to get him out of jail?" "We'll just borrow him," he said. And they did. He and Sterling Brown left the house immediately and went to the jail and asked the jailer if they could "borrow" Big Boy for the rest of the evening; they promised they would return him as soon as they had finished. The jailer knew the integrity of Edward Spencer and thus went along with the request without hesitation. Shortly afterwards, to the amazement of those gathered at 1313 Pierce that night, Edward and Sterling returned with Big Boy Davis and they played and sang and listened to Big Boy play and sing until late into the night, when they returned him to jail. This practice was later repeated.

Mrs. Spencer recalled that out of this experience (or one similar) Sterling Brown got the seed for one of his poems published in *Southern Road* (1932), "Odyssey of Big Boy." The poem itself is less a poem about Big Boy Davis than it is a transcription or adaptation of one of his songs. It has a touch of the blues form, with the repetitive last two lines of each five-line stanza slightly varied. In this poem Brown captures the heart of a type of black character once common in the South: the box-picking black man who would croon his weary blues for hours without end. Brown was interested in folklore and the southern black character of this type. Initially, he, "a northerner," relied on the Spencers'

familiarity with the area and its people to become better ac-
quainted with the myth and lore of southern blacks.

Anne Spencer said that she had a reputation for not answer-
ing letters. "But I answered every letter I ever received, though
at times—too many times—that answer did not get on the paper or in the mail." In her Notebooks are several letters which
were drafted but never mailed. There also are a few which probably were not intended to be sent, and some of these are mental notes, verse letters to her friends—as is one to Langston
Hughes:

> Dear Langston,
>
>> and *that* is what my days
>> have brought . . .
>> and this: lamp, odorless oil
>> round its long
>> dried wick:
>> Hope without wings
>> Love itself contemned
>> Where Michael broods,—
>> Arc after arc, you see,
>> If any where I own
>> A circle it is one
>> frustrate beginning—

Anne Spencer's friendship with Langston Hughes crystallized
in the mid-1920s, and she ever maintained a special fondness
for him. More than any of her literary friends, Hughes allowed
her to be herself, she said. She always was modest about her
writings and abilities, and thought that many of her literary
friends overpraised her accomplishments. But Hughes would
just let her alone, temper his praise, and keep her in touch with
the outside world by sending cards, letters, and clippings from
all over the world. Many times they exchanged poems for mutual criticism.[2] James Weldon Johnson and others of her literary
friends also solicited her critical appraisal, but Mrs. Spencer

2. Langston Hughes to Anne Spencer, February 20, 1928, in the Chauncey
E. Spencer Papers, Bentley Historical Library, Ann Arbor, Michigan.

probably was more reserved in this practice than the writers with whom she exchanged letters. She always was very partial to her writings, and for the most part only showed them to or allowed them to be published by Johnson. However, Hughes and several other writers who visited 1313 Pierce spent many hours with Anne Spencer discussing literature and perfecting their manuscripts in the relaxed atmosphere of the Spencers' house and garden.

Whether they overpraised her or not, many of these writers welcomed Anne Spencer's criticism of their works and showed a high regard for her editorial talents. Anne (Mrs. Chauncey) Spencer, her daughter-in-law, who lived with the Spencers at 1313 Pierce in the early 1940s, commented about this practice of watching Mrs. Spencer and her friends work on a manuscript until the early hours of the morning and said that Mrs. Spencer "wrote many things which were published without her name attached to them." Though Mrs. Spencer minimized such influence on her friends, she made such statements as follow when discussing a particular writer or work: that poem was written on that table over there; the manuscript for this book was mailed from this house; the original draft for that poem (or book) is upstairs now; I read that work long before it was published; he got the idea for that poem (or book) when we were doing (or discussing) this; we talked about that idea (for a poem or book) long before it was written down. Implicit here, then, is a mutual exchange of literary ideas—if not influence. And, whether or not she had a significant influence on these writers during and after the period of the Harlem Renaissance, her association with them, collectively and individually, produced a marked change in her life in Lynchburg.

Mrs. Spencer had very limited associations with local Lynchburg writers. From articles in the local newspapers and from other sources, local citizens were aware since the 1920s of the national attention she received as a published poet, but on very few occasions did Anne Spencer participate in the activities of local poetry societies. "When I'm there, I attack," she said, ex-

plaining an obvious reason why there was not a close association between her and the poetry groups in Lynchburg. Nevertheless, her association with the seminary had made her well
known in Lynchburg's black community before she became a
published poet, and her exposure in national publications
moved her more readily into the intellectual life of Lynchburg in
general, leading her into contact with whites who otherwise
might not have been aware of her existence. Martha Rivers
Adams, for many years on the staff of the local newspaper, was
attracted to Mrs. Spencer as a result of this exposure. The paper
itself called the town's attention to her "national note" on more
than one occasion after it pointed out her achievement in an article titled "Lynchburg Has Two Negro Poets of National Note"
(Lynchburg *News*, February 3, 1924).

Her closest association with a Lynchburg writer was with
Murrell Edmunds (who for many years now has been living in
New Orleans). Their contact began in the late 1920s. In her
Notebooks she listed Edmunds with a few others who, she
wrote, "more than any others in Lynchburg helped move my
life into the sun." Edmunds, still an active writer, is the author
of several novels, short stories, poems, and at least one play.
"He has always been very precious to me and Pop," Mrs. Spencer said. She asked that I call attention to his poem "Ghetto
Night" as his realization of racial matters (published in his collection of poems, *Dim Footprints Along a Hazardous Trail*, 1971).[3]

The familiar personages with whom Anne Spencer was associated were numerous, but of all the people she met who were
connected with the arts or in the public eye, of all her lifelong
friends, James Weldon Johnson held a special place in her heart.
In several of her letters to Johnson she addressed him as "Gem,"
an indication of the value she placed on his friendship. It is difficult to describe that friendship, for Mrs. Spencer often would
not allow her conversations about Johnson to reach a very personal plane. In an undated letter written probably in the fall

3. Murrell Edmunds, *Dim Footprints Along a Hazardous Trail* (New York:
A. S. Barnes and Co., 1971).

of 1933 (since in the same letter she says that she is reviewing his autobiography, *Along This Way* [1933], for a November 24 Teachers Club publication) she wrote to Johnson: "Truth is, I've been having a sort of reverent feeling toward you that I must get rid of at once."[4] But Mrs. Spencer experienced the same sort of "tears of joy and love" for her spiritual friend Johnson as she did when she spoke of Edward. "Jim," Mrs. Spencer often said, "brought my life to vibrant being. We were *friends*—and that means eternally—after our first meeting. From the first we were Jim and Anne to each other. Grace [his wife] did then and still maintains a sense of formality—but she is like that with most people; she still writes 'Dear Mrs. Spencer' even today. But Jim and I were always Jim and Anne. You know, someone once said —maybe Kant?—that you could open a can and release a whole world. That's what Jim did for me. He released my soul."

During our conversations she mentioned several times in passing that she had recorded comments about Johnson in her Notebooks. But of the materials she would show to me on occasion, she was careful not to show her notes about Johnson. To her these were among her most private and sacred thoughts, written only for herself, as were notes and poems which she wrote about her husband, her immediate family, and the Dixies. A few times when we were sifting through some materials I noticed Mrs. Spencer would come across a letter or note about Johnson (and at times about her husband and family) which she would quietly and carefully retrieve from the material and tuck away, as if by mistake these very private writings had been placed among her more general papers.

Since recording her thoughts was a lifelong practice, it would seem more than mere conjecture to say that she wrote several things specifically about Johnson. She mentioned having written shortly after his death, at the request of Grace Johnson, a poem in tribute to him, "A Mood in Memory." It is unlikely that

4. Anne Spencer to James Weldon Johnson, undated, in James Weldon Johnson Memorial Collection of Negro Arts and Letters, Collection of American Literature, Beinecke Rare Book and Manuscript Library, Yale University.

she allowed this poem to be published, if indeed she even gave it to Mrs. Johnson. Yet she did write one poem about Johnson which she sent to Mrs. Johnson and later allowed to be published, though "For Jim, Easter Eve" is no doubt less personal and less explicit than "A Mood in Memory." To my knowledge, this was her last poem to be published during her life.

This is a characteristic Anne Spencer poem: set in a garden world and articulating the spiritual solace the speaker reaps from this world of nature. Here the elegiac tone and theme elevate it above a typical occasional poem and enrich its meaning.

> For Jim, Easter Eve
>
> If ever a garden was a Gethsemane,
> with old tombs set high against
> the crumpled olive tree—and lichen,
> this, my garden has been to me.
> For such as I none other is so sweet:
> Lacking old tombs, here stands my grief,
> and certainly its ancient tree.
>
> Peace is here and in every season
> a quiet beauty.
> The sky falling about me
> evenly to the compass . . .
> What is sorrow but tenderness now
> in this earth-close frame of land and sky
> falling constantly into horizons
> of east and west, north and south;
> what is pain but happiness here
> amid these green and wordless patterns,—
> indefinite texture of blade and leaf:
>
> Beauty of an old, old tree,
> last comfort in Gethsemane.

The poem has many of the trappings of an elegy: a pastoral setting; an initial expression of intense grief and sorrow (achieved metaphorically with the allusion to Gethsemane); no mention of the person's name in the text of the poem; a final resignation to the death. The thematic movement is from intense grief in the first stanza to comfort and reconciliation in the second stanza, where grief and beauty are juxtaposed to compress the theme. Sorrow becomes tenderness, pain becomes happiness with the soothing powers of nature. The movement from grief to reconciliation is smooth and swift. Using a Christian motif, the poet is comforted by the fact that Christ's death was not a finality; it was a new beginning, an elevation of the soul. Suggesting a parallel in the second stanza between the mission of Christ as mankind's savior and the place Johnson held in her own life, the poet achieves solace with the assurance of her soul's resurrection. Peace returns and joy pervades. That Anne Spencer considered her acquaintance with "Gem" as an act of Providence, "an act of God," she often said, is readily acceptable within the context of this poem.

It was twenty years after Johnson first met Anne Spencer and helped bring her "life to vibrant being" that he was killed in an automobile accident in 1938, shortly after leaving 1313 Pierce. Two items among her memorabilia which she probably cherished most were the last postcard she received from Johnson and the telegram informing her of his death in 1938. His death brought yet another significant change to Anne Spencer's life. She withdrew somewhat from that public literary world which for twenty years had been a dominating factor in her life. Now nearing the age of sixty, yet physically and mentally as alert as ever, she became more that "private person" Arthur P. Davis noted.[5] She did not completely isolate herself—her friends still flocked to 1313 Pierce—but in many ways she participated less and less in affairs outside her home.

A few years after Johnson's death, Carl Van Vechten began collecting materials for the James Weldon Johnson Memorial Collection at Yale University Library and wrote Anne Spencer for her correspondence with Johnson. Van Vechten also invited

5. The term appears in a headnote to Anne Spencer's poems in Arthur P. Davis and Saunders Redding (eds.), *Cavalcade: Negro American Writing from 1760 to the Present* (Boston: Houghton Mifflin Co., 1971), 269. A professor of English at Howard University since 1944, Arthur Davis has distinguished himself as critic, professor, and scholar. Mrs. Spencer said that she had had a friendship with Professor Davis for several years.

her to submit her own manuscripts for the collection and brought up the subject of her writings in general. She sent selected (and edited) letters from Johnson and some of her own manuscripts. Van Vechten accepted the correspondence but rejected Mrs. Spencer's manuscripts. In a letter to me dated June 1, 1971, Mrs. Spencer stated: "In the hunt for things not seen for years, came across this paper which explains what Mr. Van Vechten did that was right. The few pieces of what were mss. were so minus and scrappy he saved me from ignominy by not submitting them." These manuscripts, which probably included several unpublished pieces, were never returned and now are supposed lost. Perhaps they were indicative of Mrs. Spencer's "scrappy" method of composition—"scribblings on bits and pieces of paper"—and therefore assumed to have little apparent value by anyone unfamiliar with her method of writing. She told Van Vechten at about the same time that she would not complete now a proposed book and story, but, she said, "at 60-odd I still have a colossal reserve of constructive indignation." [6] Interest in having her writings published appeared to cease with Johnson's death, though she continued to write, devoting her time more to prose than to poetry.

6. Anne Spencer to Carl Van Vechten [June 16, 1943?], in the Carl Van Vechten Collection, Collection of American Literature, Beinecke Rare Book and Manuscript Library, Yale University.

6 ❧ A Social Heretic

When her children arrived at college age, Anne Spencer "took a job in the Jim Crow library" to supplement the family's income. The Spencers lived comfortably on Edward's salary, but additional income would prevent undue financial strains on the family, since the three children were close enough in age to be in college about the same time. Mrs. Spencer was determined that her children would not have to get that kind of southern education which she abhorred, and which many blacks who were fortunate enough to get to college at all had to settle for. She had decided shortly after 1910 to send her children to the North for their college education, and learned then that education outside the South was more expensive. Though she had no formal training for it, she decided to apply for a job as a librarian. Books were her first love and she would feel competent and comfortable working as a librarian. But money was a secondary concern. It is likely that she decided to apply for a job in the library before she decided to earn money, for the urge to have better access to books outweighed the desire for additional income.

Whichever decision came first, one morning she dressed in her "finest red dress for business occasions," donned all the proper accessories, put a book under her arm and began the walk to Jones Memorial Library, two miles from her home. (She walked, rather than patronize Jim Crow transportation.) It was in early December of 1923 and the book she "tucked" under her arm was James Weldon Johnson's *The Book of American Negro Poetry* (1922), which contained five of her poems. Having no other credentials to recommend her for the position, she showed the librarian the poems, thinking, correctly, that a published poet would have a fairly good chance of getting a position in the library.

Soon afterwards, the board of trustees for the private (white) Jones Memorial Library met and decided to hire Anne Spencer to work at a branch of Jones to be set up in the black Dunbar High School. It may be that she actually worked for a while in the Jones Library itself before going to the Dunbar extension, for on one occasion Mrs. Spencer stated that when she acquired the job at Jones she was not a full librarian; her job was to get books from the shelves but she could not check them out to patrons. Her job at Jones, however, made her the first (and for many years the only) black allowed to use the central library's facilities. I have been unable to examine official records at Jones concerning this job. A librarian told me that the library's minutes for March, 1923, state: " 'that we approve and get a librarian at Dunbar'; the minutes don't mention her name." The trustee's minutes for January, 1924, record that the salary (figures were not made available to me) was approved for a librarian named Anne Spencer; and for February, 1924, the records show that the Dunbar branch had been open for seventeen days. The Lynchburg *News* for Sunday morning, February 3, 1924, in an article about two Lynchburg poets of national note, records that "Anne Bethel Scales Spencer has just been appointed librarian at the Jones Memorial Library extension at Dunbar High School."

Anne Spencer's ultimate aim was no doubt to desegregate the Jones Library so that black patrons would be allowed to check out books. If she actually proposed this to the library officials, it probably was not warmly received. The trustees of Jones did, however, subsidize a room in the black Dunbar High School for which it bought and furnished books otherwise unavailable to black Lynchburg readers until the local board of education took over the operation of the Dunbar branch.

Before 1924 there was not a library in Lynchburg that black patrons could use. Public library facilities for blacks in the South before about 1940 or 1950 were extremely limited. Even library facilities at black institutions of higher education were in general poorly equipped. In 1925 Monroe N. Work's *Negro Year Book* (recording data for 1924) listed twenty-one public libraries for blacks located in the South, the East, and the Midwest. Three of these were in Virginia: Norfolk, Roanoke, and Lynchburg. Since Lynchburg made the list, one can imagine the shortcomings of other public libraries for blacks at this time, for in 1925 the "library" for blacks at Dunbar was more name than fact.

"This was more a room at Dunbar than a school library," Mrs. Spencer said. But after going to Dunbar, Anne Spencer immediately began to shape the "room" into a functioning library. She contributed many of her own books and pressed Jones to do more than it perhaps otherwise would have done. She said that Jones was considerate in providing for the Dunbar branch, and she suspected that officials at Jones preferred to grant her requests for materials rather than to have her wage a campaign to desegregate Jones. When the local board of education took over the operation of the Dunbar library, it was not so easy to get needed materials, Mrs. Spencer said.

To her surprise, Jones Library paid her seventy-five dollars per month for her services. Wages were low then, especially for a black woman, and seventy-five dollars per month was a good salary. Mrs. Spencer hated what she had to do—"the Jim Crow part of it"—but she did it. For about twenty years she was head of the program at Dunbar. Though she detested being a part of segregated practices, through her efforts in this case many black readers were given access to books which they could not have obtained easily elsewhere. She minimized her role in and effect on the intellectual life of the black community in Lynchburg, but testimony has it that she introduced many students to books and sparked the desire in them to continue their education after high school. She quickly became and remained a dynamic (and controversial) figure at Dunbar High School.

Anne Spencer was a good librarian, and those now at Jones who worked with her or remember her work speak highly of her as a person and as a librarian. Even when not in the Jones facility, she often helped the other librarians with her vast knowledge, general and specific, by providing information and doing research for its patrons. Lucille Dickerson, at one time librarian at Jones, some years ago wrote a letter to Mrs. Spencer (the undated letter is among Mrs. Spencer's personal papers) which typically expressed the regard the library had for her talent:

> I appreciate so very much all the research you did for the Library. The patron for whom I wanted the data was doubly pleased.
>
> I always feel guilty when I call upon you as you go to extra trouble, however. I for the Library do thank you for your wonderful assistance at all times.

Working at Dunbar High School as a full-time librarian and occasionally as a substitute teacher, Anne Spencer conducted regular library classes in which she helped students explore the world of books and guided them in their reading. Mrs. Spencer demonstrated over and over her interest in the education of all children, but especially black children in Lynchburg: her willingness to teach at Virginia Seminary without pay when the school was in need; her campaign to oust white teachers from the black Jackson High School; her outspoken opposition to tokenism when school integration came to Lynchburg; her efforts to start and maintain a functioning library to serve blacks in the community; and her constant admonishments of those responsible for the school system in Lynchburg.

Once she joined the public school system, she discovered that there was little reading material for children, especially for black children; and in the late 1920s she wrote to W. E. B. Du Bois, hoping he would do something about it.[1] Shortly thereafter she wrote Johnson, telling him of her entreaties to Du Bois, and of his promise to do something about the problem. It seems that at the time Johnson was preparing a new book and Mrs. Spencer asked him to include in it a section for children. She reminded

1. Her letter to Du Bois is not available. But see Du Bois' comments on this in Herbert Aptheker (ed.), *The Correspondence of W. E. B. Du Bois: Volume I, Selections, 1877–1934* (Amherst: University of Massachusetts Press, 1973), 372–73.

him of the works of Mary Effie Lee Newsome: "Mrs. Newsome has written enough to fill a book or so: see her 'Black Dreams' or 'Black Boy Dreams' in October 27 *Crisis*." [2] Mrs. Newsome and Mrs. Spencer were close acquaintances until they lost contact a few years before Mrs. Spencer's death. A minor though somewhat prolific black American writer of light verse and prose, Mrs. Newsome published widely in the *Crisis* in the 1920s and 1930s, and much of her work could be especially useful for children. In the same letter Mrs. Spencer spoke of such writers of children's literature as A. A. Milne and Walter De la Mare, "who don't get beneath the surface."

One day at school while Mrs. Spencer was conducting an exercise with some small children whom she was trying to teach rudimentary techniques of literature and especially of poetry, she wrote the short poem now titled "Dunbar." Some time after this she sent the poem enclosed with a letter to Johnson who, after reading it, responded: "As soon as I opened it and found the little poem on [Paul Laurence] Dunbar, I immediately took the lines over to the *Crisis* office. They wanted very much to print the poem under Dunbar's picture in the June number, but found it was too late as the forms had been locked up." [3] He added that they would surely try to print it in another issue, which they did (November, 1920). It was also included in Countee Cullen's anthology of black poetry, *Caroling Dusk* (1927). This incident not only reveals Anne Spencer's interest in introducing children to literature but it also suggests that the scarcity of literature for children motivated her to write, as is evidenced by several drafts of verses and stories which could have been written for such a purpose. The anecdote more specifically dates the composition of the poem and attests to her early poetic activity: the "children" for whom the poem was written had to be those at the seminary when she worked there on two separate occasions between 1910

2. Anne Spencer to James Weldon Johnson, undated, in James Weldon Johnson Memorial Collection of Negro Arts and Letters, Collection of American Literature, Beinecke Rare Book and Manuscript Library, Yale University.
3. James Weldon Johnson to Anne Spencer, May 25, 1920.

and 1912, since the poem was published before she went to Dunbar as librarian and as substitute teacher.

Anne Spencer was well known, if not notorious, in certain areas of Lynchburg life before she became a published poet, for by the 1920s her unconventional behavior—whether waging a boisterous and ferocious battle against the town's Jim Crow practices or defying social decorum and sporting avant-garde fashions—had attracted the attention of whites and blacks in the town and surrounding areas. When in the 1920s and 1930s the local paper ran a few articles about her national recognition as a poet, her name became even better known in the town— one might say her national "fame" enhanced her local notoriety.

One of the events which brought her to the forefront of local attention happened shortly after World War I. For several years she had been working within the black community to improve the lot of local blacks in general, as her successful efforts to help organize a local NAACP chapter indicate. But what brought her more readily to the attention of whites in Lynchburg, according to her son Chauncey, was the movement she initiated to oust white teachers from the local black high school. The student body of Jackson High School was black, but a large number of the faculty members (if not all of them) were white, whereas black teachers went unemployed. Anne Spencer began writing letters to the local paper and to those persons who had direct influence over the school's operation, stating that the situation should be changed, that the white teachers should be removed and black teachers hired—since it was a Jim Crow school anyway. It was not that she objected to white teachers teaching black students; but since black teachers were deprived of jobs as a result of this practice, and since these same teachers were not allowed to teach in the white schools, she believed the situation, obviously unfair, should be corrected immediately. In addition to her own letters, she organized a forceful campaign within the black community to bombard the paper and public offices concerned with education with letters supporting this action. Noting that the movement was successful, Chauncey Spencer remembers that for the school year 1919–1920 black teachers replaced white teachers in Jackson High School, though the white principal remained in charge. Ostensibly this effective, organized letter writing campaign caused many people in later years to accuse Mrs. Spencer of ghostwriting letters to the paper submitted under the names of other blacks. Prior to the mid-1950s, it seems that few people in Lynchburg would expect a black citizen other than Anne Spencer (and a few others) to be courageous enough to voice dissent and indignation concerning the racially restrictive practices of the town.

Through both public and private movements Anne Spencer fought Jim Crow in Lynchburg. She began her own one-woman boycott of segregated public facilities in the early decades of this century. She refused to ride segregated public transportation and would walk, take a taxi, or just stay at home before she would spend her money to support Jim Crow. And she would not allow her children to ride segregated public transportation.

But there were occasions when she did ride the Jim Crow trolleys in defiance of segregation. One notable instance she mentioned was an occasion when she and her sister-in-law needed to go from Pierce Street to the downtown area and could not find ready transportation. They decided to take the trolley. Instead of going to the area reserved for blacks when they entered the trolley, Mrs. Spencer and her sister-in-law sat in the section reserved for whites. Infuriated, the conductor immediately asked them to move. They refused. The man became verbally abusive and one of the nicer epithets he called the two ladies was "nigger washerwomen." Recalling the incident, Mrs. Spencer said that she and her sister-in-law were dressed immaculately; they had to be for the errand they were on. But all the man's epithets and verbal abuses did not displace them from their seats. Arriving at their destination, the two went about their business. But this was not the end of the matter. As soon as her business was completed, Mrs. Spencer stormed into the office of the man who managed the trolley operations and voiced her protest. Practically as soon as she burst into the private office and began her chastisement, she recalled, the man said "You must be that Ed Spencer's wife." In fiery language, she told him how insulted she was by the conductor's abuse of them and that she would not stand for it. When she had vented her anger somewhat, she stormed out of the office. This type of open and active defiance of public segregation was a sustained effort in her life—and she willingly confronted the repercussions.

Scorning Jim Crow transportation, Anne Spencer had to find other means of getting around town, and often these other means caused her to be criticized by her neighbors for exhibiting "scandalous behavior," to use her son's term. She often hitched a ride on some of the grocery wagons in the community. Many times this was a means of getting from one place to another; at other times it was just for fun. She would jump on the back of a passing wagon and ride for a short distance or, even worse, she augmented this "scandalous behavior" by riding up front on the seat with the driver. It is quite possible that knowing she created such controversy by "acting in a way not becoming a respectable lady," she often did such things partly out of spite, to reassert her personal freedom, to show her friends and neighbors that they should not and could not dictate her modes of behavior. Such behavior, among other unconventional acts, caused her neighbors at times to "brand her as a loose woman," her son recalls. Anne Spencer paid little attention to such remarks and continued to act out of independence. Time has shown how innocent this behavior was.

It was just such neighborly reactions as these to her behavior which caused her to write the short poem "Neighbors":

> Ah, you are cruel;
> You ask too much;
> Offered a hand, a finger-tip,
> You must have a soul to clutch.

The "too much" the neighbors asked was to dictate the life of a free spirit, to restrain even further the liberties of a human being who as a result of malice and tradition was already too arbitrarily limited in social freedom.

On other occasions the ladies of the community rose to scorn her. Anne Spencer was a fashion setter, of a sort, and sported "indecent fashions" long before they became popular. For example, as often as she desired she wore such "disgraceful things as pants." Of course at the time she could not buy these outfits in the store; so she had her seamstress make them. Chauncey remembers that his mother once created quite a commotion among the black ladies in the community with her "outrageous, indecent, and scandalous attire": she wore a pants suit to a community picnic.

Her neighbors' cruelty, in their love for gossip, provided the frame for another of her short poems, "Innocence." A young girl in the community "got into trouble" and the local gossips seemed to gloat over the girl's misfortune, for, as the poem states, it was "just what the villagers lusted for." Scorned by society, the young lady seemed to degenerate until finally she died (at least in the poem). Commenting on the cruelties of "neighborly gossip," Mrs. Spencer said, "Some women are witches—and you can rhyme that with any word you want."

She said often that "'do your own thing' is right out of Emerson; and people now think they have discovered something new." In 1899 she had received a set of Emerson's works for a graduation present, which she read closely. One can see how thoroughly she absorbed the Emersonian philosophy and relied on her own conscience as to what was right and wrong, for since about 1900 she seemed to live out her personal adaptation of the teachings of Emerson's writings.

Always asserting to the fullest extent possible her rights as a free human being who adhered to few societal constraints, Anne Spencer could be called an individualist but never a selfish person. She viewed her personal struggle for human liberty as closely aligned with the struggle of all deprived and disadvantaged people. The joy she derived from her own freedom as a human being was conducive to her ceaseless efforts to fight for the human and civil liberties of others and to break down systematic social, political, and civil restraints. In such a socially and racially antagonistic town as she saw Lynchburg to be, her fight for human rights naturally manifested itself in a dedicated drive for civil and social justice for black people.

That Anne Spencer was an initiator, an organizer, and a fighter for human rights for others as well as for herself has been substantiated by many who knew her. She helped organize black citizens in Lynchburg and helped establish a local NAACP chapter about 1918. When she went to work at Dunbar in the mid-1920s, she had less time for community activist activities. Within a few years after its formation, the local NAACP chapter lost some of its effectiveness in the community and the national headquarters became worried. The head office, in its attempt to rejuvenate the Lynchburg branch, called on Anne Spencer to get things started again. The director of branches for the organization wrote her accordingly in 1926:

> As you are aware, Mr. Johnson is going to be in Lynchburg March 20–22nd. Our branch in Lynchburg has been dormant for sometime, and I am wondering whether I could impose on you the task of getting together a group of representative people that Mr. Johnson might place before them the reorganization of the branch.
>
> I realize that you do not have much time between now and his visit, but the National Office would greatly appreciate it if you could render us this service. [4]

Mrs. Spencer said that she did what she could to revive the organization in Lynchburg.

Though she praises the Virginia countryside in her poem "Life-Long, Poor Browning," she was filled with contempt for Lynchburg, for Virginia, and for the South in general. Many years ago in a letter to James Weldon Johnson she spoke of an illness, and wittily inserted: "I resented dying without your knowing I'd been ill and discouraged—'way down here in the 'total immersion belt.'" [5] The irony and sarcasm of her letters in which she spoke of Lynchburg are particularly notable. In an-

4. Robert W. Bagnall to Anne Spencer, March 15, 1926, in Spencer Family Papers, Anne Spencer House and Garden Historic Landmark, Lynchburg, Virginia.

5. Anne Spencer to James Weldon Johnson, Saturday, undated.

other letter to Johnson she wrote for its heading: "Lynchburg, and too bad at that." At other times she referred to her home town variously as "Lynchville" or "Lynch-burg," taking the opportunity to voice her disgust at the town's name. It often is said in the area that Lynchburg is named after its many lynchings; some have come to associate this with the lynchings of blacks in the area and the inherent racism which plagued the town for so many years. Actually, the town is named after John Lynch; it was settled largely by Quakers in 1757 at a ferry John Lynch established there. Another Virginian, Charles "Judge" Lynch, was notorious during the American Revolution for his sentencing many people to death by hanging. He became popularly known as the "hanging judge." It is understandable that the two—John Lynch and "Judge" Lynch—have become confused in local legend, and that the lynchings ordered by Charles Lynch in the eighteenth century have become confused with the lynchings of blacks during a much later period.

Anne Spencer realized early in her activist adult life that she alone could not completely alter the deep-rooted racism in the South, in Virginia, or in Lynchburg, especially since she had to fight both blacks and whites on this issue. Yet she never was deterred. At one time, probably after having infuriated the black population (or "black leaders") in Lynchburg, she wrote to Johnson: "I daren't show my freckles on our Main Street." [6] Responding in 1942 to a request by Carl Van Vechten that she place her materials in the James Weldon Johnson Memorial Collection, Mrs. Spencer sent them to Harold Jackman and included in the cover letter: "Will you thank Mr. Van Vechten and if you don't know why I say *thank*, try living in a place called Lynchburg for awhile." [7] In a letter to Van Vechten in 1943 Mrs. Spencer

6. Anne Spencer to James Weldon Johnson, Thursday, November 9, undated.

7. Anne Spencer to Harold Jackman, July 1, 1942, in the James Weldon Johnson Memorial Collection of Negro Arts and Letters. Harold Jackman was closely associated with the intellectual circles of the Harlem Renaissance groups. Born in London, he came to the United States as a child. He was a 1923 graduate of New York University and held a master's degree from Columbia University. For more than thirty years he taught in the New York public schools. As a collector of memorabilia, he contributed to collections of black arts and letters at Atlanta University, Yale University, Fisk University, and the Schomburg Collection of the New York Public Library. He died in 1961.

reminisced about her early battles with Lynchburg: "[In] 1917–8 when I first knew 'Mr. Johnson,' I was straining to escape Lynchburg without realizing I might just 'take over'—silly still!" [8]

Even before integration became a major issue in the 1950s, Mrs. Spencer's views and outspoken opinions on the race question branded her a radical among and by blacks. In 1930, frustrated and angry with local blacks, she wrote to Johnson: "My forty-eighth birthday finds me galvanized into an obsession that has been a long time flowing in: A vile indignation for and against Niggers! I love and hate 'em; dreaming, waking, it's all one—my Phantom 'Rickshaw.' Oh, to be able to succor or destroy them in one God-like motion! See, and pardon, the ebullition a few left-handed phrases from you released. The locale, Sir, is to blame." [9]

Those in a position to know, including Anne Spencer, have preferred not to talk at length about her battles with Lynchburg society during a twenty-five year period beginning about 1930. Those who did relate specific incidents (again including Mrs. Spencer) asked that this material remain confidential or be treated with the utmost discretion, since it involved too many people. Some persons, however, provided general comments indicative of Anne Spencer as the unreformed social heretic of Lynchburg.

In a letter to me (November 7, 1972) Murrell Edmunds commented on the fact that Mrs. Spencer seldom published anything which might reveal her personal reactions to the racial problems in Lynchburg: "Moreover, you must remember that both Mrs. Spencer and her husband held jobs in a tight 'whiteman' dominated society and so were particularly vulnerable to attack from whatever defender of the status quo who might have been around. So she, who was so strictly disciplined, would not go out of her way to reveal her feelings at so deep a level. I do not mean that she was a passive or negative personality. Far from it. She was her own person, calm and self-contained and independent."

8. Anne Spencer to Carl Van Vechten, June 24, 1943, in the Carl Van Vechten Collection, Collection of American Literature, Beinecke Rare Book and Manuscript Library, Yale University.

9. Anne Spencer to James Weldon Johnson, January 29, 1930.

Though Mrs. Spencer worked in a black school, the position probably was one that traditionally would have been given to a white. Edward Spencer's job was that of Lynchburg's first parcel postman, which created some unpleasant incidents. When in 1913 the local post office asked for bids to carry parcel post, Edward Spencer's bid was the lowest; he got the job. With a mule-drawn wagon which he enclosed on all sides and painted red, white, and blue—to be sure, from the description this was an early version of the present-day local mail van—Edward Spencer delivered parcel post for the Lynchburg post office until he retired in 1943. The position traditionally would have been reserved for whites; the result was that more than once he was subjected to racial abuse. Several whites complained that Edward would not come to the back doors of their homes when delivering packages. Shortly after he obtained the job, a prominent white citizen complained to the Lynchburg postmaster about "that nigger who walks up to my door just like a white man." He asked the postmaster to inform Mr. Spencer that blacks were not allowed at his front door, and that Mr. Spencer must deliver all parcels only at his back door. He vowed, Chauncey Spencer recalls, that "that nigger will never come to my front door again." Edward Spencer was just as defiant of Jim Crow as his wife, and stated that he was not a back-door postman. The Lynchburg postal department supported Mr. Spencer's determination never to deliver mail to a back door when the mail box or usual place of delivery was at the front. Both Mr. Spencer and the complaining citizen stood firm: Mr. Spencer never delivered a package to the house again; the man had to receive his packages at the post office.

The range of racial problems the Spencers (especially Anne) faced during that 1930 to 1955 period (for which I have little information) are intriguing because of the hesitancy of some of the witnesses and the implications raised by the comments of others. Dr. Ben Fuson (a Robert Browning scholar, a former resident of Lynchburg, and professor at Lynchburg College in the 1940s) and his family were among a select few who, Mrs. Spencer recorded in her Notebooks, "more than any others in Lynch-burg helped move [her] life into the sun." Professor Fuson re-called for me his first acquaintance with Anne Spencer:

I'd known a couple of her fine poems from the J. W. Johnson old an-thology, but we'd not realized she lived in our community. My wife and I and our children Linda, 7, and David, 6, ventured to visit 1313 Pierce. Anne met us at door with great wariness and reserve, but when we mentioned the author's name as talisman she swept out her arms and warmly welcomed us in. We'd meant to stay only 20 minutes, but were there for a wonderful two hours and fell in love with Anne com-pletely, also finding her husband Edward a fine and sensitive hus-band. The unique old house with its inlaid parquet flooring and space crowded with momentos and books and magazines et al fascinated us also, and the wonderful back garden was also a treat to stroll in.

We visited her again several times, if I recall correctly, before leaving Lynchburg in 1948, and urged her to come see us at our home near Lynchburg College, but Anne always refused with dignity—we under-stood that she'd been treated with racial slurs in earlier venturings out, and of course also felt acutely the Lynchburg put-downs of Negroes in general, and would not expose herself to such traumas again. [10]

Lynchburg did not allow Anne Spencer to challenge its racial and social traditions with impunity. Between about 1930 and 1955, defenders of the status quo often branded those who spoke out against racial and social injustice as Communists, with all the connotations and consequences attached to such a label at that time. More than one person has stated that it is highly likely Anne Spencer was suspected of having close links with Com-munists at one time. Such accusations, whether true or false, could have accounted for the heightened antagonism toward her at one time (perhaps that 1930 to 1955 period in particular), and the verbal abuses often directed against her when she was in some public sector of the town. Mrs. Spencer herself spoke of an FBI agent's visiting her in connection with one of her closest friends in Lynchburg, Bernice Lomax Hill.

Ms. Hill, before her death in 1970, was probably Anne Spen-cer's dearest friend. Mrs. Spencer said they had a meeting of the

10. Ben Fuson to author, March 3, 1974.

minds and many times would sit and talk until the early hours of the morning. Ms. Hill taught for several years in the public schools of Lynchburg. When she applied for a job abroad with the federal government, she faced some difficulties. She was an exceptionally bright woman, an excellent teacher, and, thinking along the lines of Anne Spencer, was not particularly liked by the local board of education. After she had applied for a teaching position abroad, the school board gave her a negative recommendation and "someone linked her with Communism." Investigating Ms. Hill's background, the FBI agent, Mr. Frieze, a resident of Lynchburg, came to question Mrs. Spencer about Ms. Hill. He found Anne Spencer in her garden. "The man asked if she had Communist connections. I stopped what I was doing and asked him to sit on the concrete bench nearby. Now, I could tell you that she's no more of a Communist than I am. But that wouldn't do you any good because you don't know *how Communist I am*. Or I could say that she's no more of a Communist than you are. You would know. I don't know but that you're a double agent." Mrs. Spencer continued in this vein and probably gave Mr. Frieze little information concerning Ms. Hill's alleged link with Communism, if indeed she did have Communist ties. Mr. Frieze remained in the garden a long time and evidently was so "interested" in Anne Spencer that he asked if he could bring his son to visit her. She quickly retorted: "I hope you don't think your son is going to get any information you didn't get!" The man did bring his son to visit; and Bernice Lomax Hill finally obtained a position in Paris teaching the children of American military officers.

Another person's recollections of Lynchburg days (probably the 1930s) provided an interesting comment on the same topic. Not knowing that Mrs. Spencer had spoken to me of the same general topic, the person cautioned that the information should be treated delicately (therefore I will not include the writer's name). Mrs. Spencer said more than once "my life is an open crook" and "I don't mind what is told concerning *me*." I believe it is clear that the following comments are observations rather than accusations:

I shall tell you of an incident which you must treat with the most delicate sense of responsibility. For anybody to hint in any way that Mrs. Spencer was a Communist, or a fellow-traveller, or even sympathetic to the party would be a baseless untruth. She never revealed the slightest interest in matters like that. . . . But, still, she was far too perceptive, too wise, to dismiss the movemet out of fear or lack of tolerance. . . . There was a young man . . . who belonged to the Communist party, and who had given himself at the time I knew him to a complete dedication to its work and objectives. . . . Once he told me of a social gathering of mixed blacks and whites which was held at Mrs. Spencer's home. I asked him what they did there, and he replied they talked and discussed things in general and danced among themselves.

That's all I know about it, and I am positive it had nothing to do with radicalism, but was rather a revealing insight into Mrs. Spencer's character—she was not about to embark on any crusades, but neither was she surrendering her right to entertain in her home whomever she wished. The social mixing of black and white in Lynchburg at that time was definitely unacceptable, and it took not only vision and wisdom, but courage far beyond the usual. As far as I could tell this was just a gathering of thoughtful members of both races for an evening of discussion and entertainment. But it has always seemed to me to indicate the strength of Mrs. Spencer's character and the calm independence of her role in society.

Later I mentioned to Mrs. Spencer this young radical's name—he was a quiet, attractive boy, deeply involved in his party activities and a very appealing man—and she said very softly, very philosophically, maybe a little sadly: "They'll get him, too." And I took that to mean that she was speaking of the fate of all those who stepped out to battle what they thought was wrong in mankind's endless succession of changes. . . . Of course she might have been thinking of what the Communists might do to him, but that was not my impression.

The effectiveness of her racial protests and chastisements depended on either a positive or negative reaction from her opponents. Finding at one time letters to her adversaries an effective means of expressing her discontent, she later had to reckon with the fact that many times her letters did not gain a response of any kind—whether from the local paper or from some administrative official or agency in the town. To remedy this, she would write letters to the editors of the local paper and dare them to be printed. When the effect of this dare method against her targets diminished, Anne Spencer resorted to personal confrontations to make herself heard. Eventually, though, those whom she provoked into some kind of reaction became immune to her attacks after her strategy became too well known. She said that after a while those who were targets of her protests—newspapers, radio stations, public officials, among others—would let her have her say and then ignore her, giving the impression that she was an eccentric who had nothing substantial to say, but because of her age and eccentricities, she would be tolerated. Her opponents, therefore, realized that of all the methods used to discredit her, none deterred or defeated her as long as she got some kind of reaction. So she found her opponents' use of neutral counterattack difficult to deal with. This is what infuriated her most, for she hated to be "tolerated" and believed any response whatsoever to her agitations was a sign of progress. Most often she learned to turn what others might consider defeat into a continuing challenge. For her outspoken provocations Anne Spencer was subjected to ostracism, personal derision, racial slurs, and generally hostile attitudes during most of her adult life in Lynchburg. Yet she endured with strength, courage, and determination. For over four decades she was certainly one of Lynchburg's most vocal and active social heretics.

7 ✂ The Poetry: Aestheticism

1975

Turn an earth clod
Peel a shaley rock
In fondness molest a curly worm
Whose *familiar* is everywhere
Kneel
And the curly worm   sentient *now*
Will *light* the word that tells the poet what a poem is

Anne Spencer wrote this poem in June, 1974. Stating then that it might be her last poem, she said that "1975" could be considered a comment on her life and writings. It was largely from the daily activities of her life that she found the settings, moods, themes, motifs, and images for her poetry. In her poetry are frequent references (though sometimes veiled) to her family, friends, and associates. A love for natural scenery in general, and especially for her garden, provided a metaphorical setting for many of her poems. From her readings in history, literature, and current events she found the germinal ideas for several of her topical poems. The statement that the "*familiar* is everywhere" when applied to her poetry borders on the mystical, for the sophisticated manner in which she approached these familiar observations of her environment allowed her to explore their meanings in uncommon depth.

At times cryptic, at other times deceptively simple,[1] her poems tell much about the inner and outer selves of the poet. A mystic she might not have been, but Anne Spencer was a vi-

1. As Sterling Brown observes in *Negro Poetry and Drama* (Washington, D.C.: The Associates in Negro Folk Education, 1937), 66.

sionary of sorts. Speaking of the theme in her sonnet "Substitution," she said that one must substitute reality to get reality; that unless we have ideas, reality is too stark. "Substitution," one of her favorite poems, is a good schematic example of the plan and themes of her poetry, as well as a partial explanation of why she wrote poetry. It begins with questioning:

> Is Life itself but many ways of thought,
> How real the tropic storm or lambent breeze
> Within the slightest convolution wrought
> Our mantled world and men-freighted seas?
> God thinks . . . and being comes to ardent things:

These opening lines deal with the power of creativity associated with God. Posing a question in the first four lines, the speaker in line five is brought to the vast and magnificent power of the Supreme Creator, who creates the world of reality in a single thought. He forms "Within [His] slightest convolution . . . /Our mantled world" and thus gives "being . . . to ardent things." He creates "The splendor of the day-spent sun, love's birth,—/ Or dreams a little, while creation swings/The circle of His mind and Time's full girth." In the octave, then, the poet draws a parallel between the creative powers of God and the poet. The poet as imitator and creator substitutes for "Our mantled world" of reality his own thinking, or dreams and thus gives "being" to "ardent things." Yet in his substitution the poet also creates other mantled worlds. God creates "The splendor of the day-spent sun"; the poet assigns the birth of love to the setting sun and, in one sense, gives it human meaning. The speaker holds that anyone can create in his own mind, that creation is not limited to God and poets. The poem answers the question posed in the first line in the affirmative: life itself is but many ways of thought. The speaker whose "thought leans forward" is then quickly "lifted clear/Of brick and frame," the real world, and creates for himself a world of "moonlit garden bloom."

In 1974 Anne Spencer revised the first five lines of "Substitution" as they originally were published:

Is Life itself but many ways of thought,
Does *thinking* furl the poets' pleiades,
Is in His slightest convolution wrought
These mantled worlds and their men-freighted seas?
He thinks—and being comes to ardent things:

Mrs. Spencer explained that she never meant to capitalize *His* in line three, and that so doing "ruined the whole poem." She revised these lines in order to improve the diction (to delete *pleiades*) and to polish the ambiguity by deleting some references to God and the poet. With *His* in the lower case, the poem as originally published would concern primarily the poet and the speaker as creators. This capitalization "error" (but one should compare *His* in line eight, as well as *poets'* instead of *poet's* in line two) shows a blending of the human and the divine as creators, an association which is characteristic of several of her poems, and which seems to work well throughout this sonnet. The grammatical and visual relationship between *poets'* and *His* creates a kind of ambiguity or double meaning which is sustained in the poem. But Mrs. Spencer believed the ambiguity in the original version hindered more than it helped. The revision may, however, make the reader work harder to glean the meaning of these lines. It also deletes in the octave the idea that the poet shares a power of creation with God, an idea which remains in the sestet. In the original version the octave asks not one question, but poses a series of at least three different yet interrelated questions about life, creation and creators, appearance and reality.

"Substitution" conveys a desire to change this world of cold, stark reality for one of beauty and love; the sestet affirms the capacity of any person to do this. And whether in her own garden or in the garden as symbol of a perfect world in her poetry, through the creative, life-giving process Anne Spencer managed to substitute a more perfect world to compensate for the imperfect society in which she lived. This was her motivation for writing poetry.

The sestet of "Substitution" begins with a topical allusion—

an example of how well she veils the subjective and topical to achieve the objective and universal. The lines "As here within this noisy peopled room/My thought leans forward," said Mrs. Spencer, refer to a courtroom scene where she witnessed the trial of a black preacher accused of murder. The man was possessed more by lust than love for a young girl, whom he murdered out of passion. This particular idea also is recorded in her Notebooks: "The test by which we can *know* we have reached the high point in human Love is not only what I will do for it, but what I absolutely refuse to do against it." On the same topic she wrote at another time: "There is always this test: The grave, even supernatural difference between love and lust is that the loving heart desires to *do* everything for its object, and nothing against it." To escape the farcical trial, to escape the unpleasant proceedings of southern justice (or injustice), the poet-speaker could and did mentally leave this world of ugliness, impurity, and hate, and substituted a visionary world of pure love and beauty. Thematically, in a large group of her poems she envisions life as a journey through a human world of suffering and pain in quest of a spiritual world of infinite peace and harmony. "1975" informs us that gleaning intimations from the familiar was the approach she took to her poetry; "Substitution" tells us how and why she wrote poetry. What follows in this chapter is a discussion of part of what she wrote.

Using "At the Carnival" and "Questing" as thematically representative poems, I can see a large group of Anne Spencer's poems forming an aesthetic or poetic *Pilgrim's Progress*. Within the group there is a rejection of a degenerate world ("At the Carnival") in quest of one of supernal beauty ("Questing"), in quest of the Celestial City which in her poetry is symbolized by the garden setting.

In her poems she seldom mentions from whence man comes before his life's quest. Her attention is focused on what in "Translation" she calls the "far country" at the end of life's journey. By focusing on this idealistic "far country" for which man quests, she necessarily draws attention to this world of reality in which we now live. The road of life is filled with ugliness, with "anvil and strife," with pain and suffering, with sorrow, with all the conditions which make the speakers of her poems strive to attain that "far country." But everything on the road of life is not negative, for there are glimmers of beauty which show us how perfect life must be in the "far country," but which make the journey through this life even more difficult because the knowledge of that ideal world reveals the imperfection of this one and fills us with yearning. The motif implies a fated philosophy: man is placed on the road of life and destined "To grope, eyes shut, and fingers touching space" ("Questing") for that almost unattainable world of pure beauty.

"At the Carnival" is one of her few poems which deals specifically with this world of reality in which we live—this "sordid life," this "unlovely thing" which practically overwhelms the glimmers of beauty. In this poem the world of reality is seen metaphorically as a carnival peopled primarily by grotesque figures and blind crowds. Those at the carnival of life, whether as participants or observers, can recognize in such fragile symbols as the diving-tank girl our hopes for redemption from this world of Vanity Fair. And though the poem concentrates on negativism, on the carnival of life, it ultimately moves to a conclusive statement of hope and affirmation (though expressed somewhat despairingly): "I implore Neptune to claim his child today!"

Anne Spencer said that she wrote "At the Carnival" long before she wrote "Before the Feast at Shushan," her first poem to be published. So "At the Carnival" probably was written shortly after 1910 or possibly as early as the turn of the century. During the early decades of this century carnivals and fairs were common throughout the South. Once Ed and Anne went to a carnival located just a few blocks from their home. Anne had been "out-of-sorts" for a few days prior to this, and Ed urged her to go with him, thinking that the carnival would provide some diversion and maybe relax her mind. She agreed, and shortly afterwards recorded the event:

> I came incuriously—
> Set on no diversion save that my mind
> Might safely nurse its brood of misdeeds
> In the presence of a blind crowd.
> The color of life was gray.
> Everywhere the setting seemed right
> For my mood!

The carnival mirrored her unsettled state of mind; it also probably mirrored the causes of her disturbance. A microcosm of this
imperfect world after Eden, the carnival is filled with the bizarre,
the ugly, the grotesque; it is full of fate and chance:

> Here the sausage and garlic booth
> Sent unholy incense skyward;
> There a quivering female-thing
> Gestured assignations, and lied
> To call it dancing;
> There, too, were games of chance
> With chances for none;

Walking through the carnival and absently gazing at all the grotesque figures "amid the malodorous/Mechanics of this unlovely thing," the speaker's attention is suddenly caught by a
gleam of beauty among all this ugliness. She notices the "Gay
little Girl-of-the-Diving-Tank" amid this "sordid life" and her
spirits are lifted. She sees in this "darling of spirit and form" a
beauty which reflects her own heart: a heart which yearns for
beauty in a world which has become ugly; a heart which invariably searches for some vestige of Eden in a world of grotesques.

The world indeed has changed since Eden. The speaker,
nursing her "brood of misdeeds," initially feels a sort of kinship
with the "blind crowd," that crowd which is so fascinated by the
grotesques of life, the freaks of nature, that it is oblivious to the
"form divine." But unlike the "blind crowd," the freaks themselves can make the contrast between their own fallen state and
the innocent beauty of the "Girl-of-the-Diving-Tank":

> My Limousine-Lady knows you, or
> Why does the slant-envy of her eye mark
> Your straight air and radiant inclusive smile?

> Guilt pins a fig-leaf; Innocence is its own adorning.
> The bull-necked man knows you—this first time
> His itching flesh sees form divine and vibrant health,
> And thinks not of his avocation.

After the Fall, man's destiny is to die. Through his sins he has forfeited perpetual life, "form divine," and "vibrant health" on this earth. To redeem himself and be assured of eternal life in another form, man must embrace the divine form of beauty here symbolized in the diving girl. By embracing her one can embrace the representative of God; the girl is goodness personified, "and/Whatever is good is God."

"At the Carnival" is singular among Anne Spencer's poems in that it concentrates on the evils and ugliness of a world for which the speakers of her various poems want to substitute a more perfect world. "Substitution" states that poetry will be the vehicle by which the poet will escape from a world morally and spiritually gone awry. The poem attests to the powers of the imagination, to the fortitude of a creative mind in search of beauty. Such an attempt to escape the sorrows of the world gives birth to poetry: "Art—a substitute for natural living—can be born either of joy or sorrow; as mother the former is very unlikely" (Notebooks). Practically all of the personae of her poems are pilgrims questing for a better life. Defying earthly and mortal obstacles placed in their paths, they tread relentlessly through this world of Vanity Fair as they seek the prize of knowledge and spiritual contentment in the Celestial City. It is her poem "Questing" which appropriately conveys this theme. "Questing" relates the urgency, the symbolic objective, the motivation, and the difficulty for the pilgrim poet:

> Let me learn now where Beauty is;
> My day is spent too far toward night
> To wander aimlessly and miss her place;
> To grope, eyes shut, and fingers touching space.

The thematic frame for the discussion of the poems which follow will be the poetic contrast between the degeneracy of this present world and the idealism of the world and life hereafter.

The simplicity of "Rime for the Christmas Baby" may cause the reader to dismiss it as a trivial occasional poem; yet it fits well into this schematic treatment of Anne Spencer's poetry. The poem is cast in the form of a letter to a friend (Bess Alexander) celebrating the birth of her baby on Christmas Day. The birth of the baby is his entry upon the journey to that "far country." His progress through this life may be hampered by mortal and non-spiritual obstacles; he may even be enticed by the false, superficial, and transient symbols of a perfect life—material possessions: "He'll have rings and linen things, / And others made of silk." But these things are transitory and unimportant when compared to what awaits him at the end of this life's journey. However, all the material and mortal possessions of this world are not negative, for "True, some sort of merit in a mart / Where goods are sold for money, / But packed with comfort is the heart / That shares with you what's funny."

We can reconcile ourselves to the "things" of this life, the superficial or even ugly things, just as the grotesques in "At the Carnival" resign themselves to what this life holds for them. Yet we understand that there is beauty in this world and something even better awaiting us, in the same way that the Limousine-Lady, the bull-necked man, and the speaker in "At the Carnival" can understand the beauty of the diving-tank girl. But there are those who cannot accept the conventionalities of life, such as the speaker in "The Wife-Woman" or the sister in "Letter to My Sister." As does the wife-woman, we might long for that "far country"; but we *must* wait, since Fate decrees it, just as it decrees that we must make this journey through life. We must, the speaker of "Rime for the Christmas Baby" says, resign ourselves to it: "So please kiss him when he's very bad / And laugh with him in gladness." It matters not how much we fret and pray; we have no control over our plight. There are forces greater than we who have fated us to make this journey: "Life is too long a way to go, / And age will bring him sadness." And though we pray for relief through death (a pervasive theme in her poetry), we must wait our fate. Life is hard, but one can earn salvation and achieve immortality in "Time's unfading garden."

Fate and chance are motifs which recur in Anne Spencer's poetry. But, although one must wait for that spiritual and physical salvation from this life, one must not be idle; one must struggle to attain that place, must be active and defiant of the earthly forces which retard progress. On one level, "Letter to My Sister" (first published in a slightly different version as "Sybil Warns Her Sister") conveys the same theme. Speaking of the poem, Anne Spencer said that although she never had a congenital sister, she had close friendships with women who came near to being congenital sisters and thus were spiritual sisters. This poem is a letter to her sisters of the world. Speaking of a major idea in the poem, Mrs. Spencer said, "You don't ever get clear of problems." Often in her poems she blends or contrasts pagan and orthodox religious motifs. Here the forces of the world which one must fight against are characterized as pagan deities. "It is dangerous for a woman to defy the gods;/To taunt them with the tongue's thin tip," for the gods are very powerful. But "worse still if you mince timidly—/Dodge this way or that, or kneel or pray." Though "the gods are Juggernaut,"

> This you may do:
> Lock your heart, then, quietly,
> And lest they peer within,
> Light no lamp when dark comes down
> Raise no shade for sun;
> Breathless must your breath come through
> If you'd die and dare deny
> The gods their god-like fun.

The poem recalls a major thematic statement in Paul Laurence Dunbar's novel *The Sport of the Gods*: whom the gods wish to destroy, they first make mad.[2] It suggests Fate operating in this world (if not a tinge of fatalism), a kind of naturalistic approach to life. Naturalistic and fatalistic overtones are to be found in a poem like "At the Carnival," but the thrust of Anne Spencer's poetry is her belief in the world that beauty gives us inklings of —intimations which we must cultivate like a garden. Thus her

2. Paul Laurence Dunbar, *The Sport of the Gods* (New York: Dodd, Mead and Co., 1902), 88.

poetry and her garden are manifestations of the same principle of creativity.

Anne Spencer's garden was central to her life; it is of primary importance in her poetry. People who knew her almost always knew of her garden; frequently they knew of the garden before they knew her. When at home as a "housewife" and after coming home from her job as Dunbar High School's librarian, she would spend most of her waking hours during the week in this garden. It was not unusual for her "to plant the thorn and kiss the rose" ("Any Wife to Any Husband") until she could no longer see how to work; then, if there was no light from the moon, she would use candles or other artificial light. When not tending the plants and flowers, many times she would retire to the garden house and absorb herself in reading and writing. It is in this setting that she composed many of her poems, taking much of her imagery and many of her metaphors directly from that garden world. The garden house not only held tools for gardening, but contained a library for her reading and writing and served as a second storehouse for her papers and literary materials. It follows, then, that many times she would collect her thoughts in the peaceful, harmonious atmosphere of the garden grounds ("Peace is here and in every season/a quiet beauty" ["For Jim, Easter Eve"]) and work on her poetry in the seclusion of the garden house. Since cultivating her garden was a major part of her day-to-day activities, it is understandable that this garden functions frequently as image, metaphor, and symbol in her poems. A short poem from her Notebooks expresses the sanctity of a garden world and man's violation of it:

> Sunday 22—'28
>> God never planted a garden
>> But He placed a keeper there;
>> And the keeper ever razed the ground
>> And built a city where
>> God cannot walk at the eve of day,
>> Nor take the morning air.

For a woman whose mental and spiritual selves were not in

harmony with her human environment, her garden was a pallia-
tive haven. In Lynchburg it became her "last comfort in Gethsemane" as she sought spiritual shelter from the town's hostile
society. Not only was it a welcome retreat from the repressive
town, but the garden also allowed her to get out of the house.
Such a withdrawal was not so much to escape her family, but
when she retired to the garden house she was freed from living
daily the traditionally exact roles of mother and wife. She needed
and desired a certain spiritual nourishment which her family
and friends could not provide her, and which she found in her
garden world of nature.

As in her life the garden was to her an otherworldly realm of
innocence, beauty, goodness, and purity, so it comes to repre-
sent Eden and the ideal realm in her poems. The contrast of the
"anvil and strife" of the real world and "Time's unfading garden" is at the heart of her poetry. The garden may also be a
Gethsemane, a place of grief, as in "For Jim, Easter Eve" where
the very beauty and perfection of the place weigh upon the poet
a sense of loss; but in most of the poems the garden conveys
ideals, such as love, beauty, immortality.

"Before the Feast at Shushan" praises the beauty of the Garden of Shushan which reflects the Garden of Eden. Natural scenery in total—grass, flowers, birds, the landscape—becomes
in her poetry an expression of beauty, whether such a natural
scene is artificially tamed (such as the Garden of Shushan or her
own garden) or wildly ordered (such as the Garden of Eden or
the Virginia countryside in "Life-Long, Poor Browning"). Garden scenery thus becomes linked with the divine, with tinges of
both pantheism and mysticism. As Eden was a creation of God,
so natural scenery is a manifestation of God's creative powers,
evidence of a divine and spiritual force in this human world. In
"Substitution" we see the poet and God as creators, and the
garden as symbolic of their creative powers. Suggested here is
the idea that within the human species there is parcel of divinity, of the spiritual, which ultimately suggests (in the thematic
scheme of her poetry, at least) that the human is capable of

achieving immortality and sharing divinity. The human poet shares with God the power of creation. In "At the Carnival" if we can see the "plodder" as another creator, one who works laboriously to create what is good and beautiful, then the gardener as "plodder" has a link with the divine. The speaker in "At the Carnival" states: "I am swift to feel that what makes/The plodder glad is good; and/Whatever is good is God." The garden, then, the landscape, is a manifestation of beauty and of whatever is good. The garden is also used as a setting for lovers. The garden at 1313 Pierce Street remained a relic of the love bond between Anne and Edward. Edward built the garden for her and helped her cultivate it, and the two traveled many miles to acquire exotic plants for the garden. Edward also built havens for animals who were housed in the garden: bird houses (for which he gained local popularity) as homes for both special and ordinary birds and a pond for fish and frogs and any other animal that could survive there. In a quiet lyric Anne Spencer expresses Edward's attitude toward his wife and her garden:

He Said:

"Your garden at dusk
Is the soul of love
Blurred in its beauty
And softly caressing;
I, gently daring
This sweetest confessing,
Say your garden at dusk
Is your soul, My Love."

Moreover, the garden becomes a sanctuary of complete bliss for all lovers for all times. The theme of immortality, of transcending the world of stark reality, is central to the conclusion of "Substitution" where the speaker and her lover enjoy a binding love relationship that is sacred because it is not of the flesh, not of this world, but is in that world of "moonlit garden bloom." (The phrase perhaps derives from the fact that Anne and Edward often planted their garden by moonlight, or spent much time there in the quiet night of the full moon.) The same poetic function of this garden scene is evident in the two poems she wrote related to her favorite poet, Robert Browning. Both poems deal with immortality and suggest the garden scene as a sacred haven for immortal lovers. In "Life-Long, Poor Browning" Anne Spencer comments on the relationship between the mortal and the divine, the earthly and the heavenly.

The poem is filled with natural imagery which builds to the "immortal completeness." Garden scenery pervades the entire poem as a comparative portrait of the wild garden scenery of the Virginia countryside, English gardens, and, metaphorically, what must be heaven. The first two stanzas describe the lush countryside of Virginia as superior to that of English gardens. The third and fourth stanzas picture the Virginia landscape as rivaling heaven. Inverting the metaphor in the middle of the poem, the poet blends the heavenly and the earthly as she praises her home state. She achieves a kind of ambiguity by describing heaven in terms of the Virginia countryside, and the garden imagery which may have both heaven and Virginia as its referent expands the original metaphor. Though the closing couplet emphasizes just where "Here" is—in heaven—the metaphor still lingers and underscores again the comparison of heaven and Virginia.

The poem laments that since "Life-long, poor Browning never knew Virginia," he perhaps never knew the beauty of heaven. But "Dead, now, dear Browning lives on in heaven." He has achieved in death what this life could not give him. Browning, as poet and creator, possessed a link with the divine and thus was entitled to immortality. But the beauty of heaven itself is not sufficient, this poem says, for Browning to enjoy a full life of immortality. Differing somewhat from the usual structure of an Anne Spencer poem (which begins with doubting or questioning and moves to an affirmation), this poem ends with a question. The question is not whether Browning is enjoying immortality (affirmed at the beginning of stanza three), but whether "Shade that was Elizabeth" is there to complete his immortal life. Pondering this particular idea at one time, she recorded in her Notebooks: "To meet again in another world is, I believe, so rare it must be one of the great accidents of the universe."

The closing question repeats somewhat differently an idea expressed near the end of "Substitution" and in other of her poems: immortal completeness implies retaining something earthly. "Substitution" assumes that both lovers will transcend this world. But "Life-Long, Poor Browning" brings this point into question and states that without reunion of man and wife (lovers) after this world, immortality would be incomplete.

"Life-Long, Poor Browning" alludes to Browning's "Home-Thoughts, From Abroad." Her second Browning poem, "Any Wife to Any Husband: A Derived Poem," based on Browning's "Any Wife to Any Husband" ("This poem sounds plagiarized to me," she said), begins: "This small garden is half my world." This opening line likely refers to her physical world in Lynchburg, for there her garden indeed was a significant part of her total world. Yet the line could refer also to something larger when read in the context of the entire poem. Judging from the canon of her poetry, one may surmise that "my world" refers to time on earth and time spent in immortality. An entry in her Notebooks perhaps provides an additional gloss on the idea: "Life, death. Apart they are half; together they are one. The mystic half of what is self. The other half death makes is lovely whole and full promise." The poem ends with a similar notion to that of "Life-Long, Poor Browning." After the speaker is dead and the husband remarries, she wishes her husband much joy in this mortal life with his new wife, but hopes that their physical joys will not lure him from a pursuit of eternal bliss.

In "Lines to a Nasturtium (A Lover Muses)" again garden scenery is indicative of the love between two people. But there is a twist here. The beauty of the woman is compared to the beauty of the nasturtium, not in metaphysical but in physical terms. Unfortunately, mere physical attraction is transitory and ultimately destructive if one fails to see the inherent spirituality behind it. In this case, that beauty which attracts—which should be a gleam of the spiritual and the eternal—destroys.

"No one could be more critical than I of my proneness to [see?] Love and the obvious in what I write," she recorded in her Notebooks. Love was sacred to Anne Spencer, and that kind of love of which she wrote—love distinguished by an eternal bond between two people—is a relationship "Less as flesh unto flesh, more as heart unto heart" ("Creed"). Another entry in her Notebooks further characterizes her attitude toward love and writers' treatment of the subject: "Women in my day (IMD) wrote weakly of love—because of excess, pardon, expatiation on the subject. They kept love in a state of infancy—and they stayed there with it." When writing about feminine love, poets seldom, said Mrs. Spencer, write about a woman who loves her mate more than she loves (or to the exclusion of) her children, though such a situation is not uncommon in life. This is the point of view she takes in "The Wife-Woman."

It was perhaps about 1918 or 1919 that she wrote "The Wife-Woman." She said that about World War I she was reading in the newspapers about a soldier who had been killed in battle, leaving at home a widow and seven children. She wondered then how the widow felt, and there began the seed for the poem. But it was not composed immediately; it was another process of her reading which gave the poem a more definite shape. She explained: "How I make a poem. I start with a word or two and begin associating." In this case she said that she was reading a passage about the Pleiades in *Crowell's Handbook for Readers and Writers*.[3] In reference to some unfinished poems and pieces of prose on which she was working, she showed me how she derived ideas for her writings from entries in this handbook. She began associating the Pleiades and their reference to sailors with the image in her mind of the wife-woman. The idea occurred to her that many people are superstitious, and that everybody

3. Mrs. Spencer said that she often had gleaned ideas for poems from reading certain entries in this handbook. But for "The Wife-Woman" she could have been mistaken, for the particular edition of *Crowell's Handbook* which I saw in her house was published in 1925, two years after the publication of "The Wife-Woman." It is possible that she was reading about the Pleiades in another book.

needs something to which he can pray. After this, the images, metaphors, and language for the poem concretized. Using the dominant theme of a never-dying wifely love, Anne Spencer interweaves the motifs of death, transcendence, and religion (superstition) in "The Wife-Woman" to express convincingly "such / Love as culture fears":

> Maker-of-Sevens in the scheme of things
> From earth to star;
> Thy cycle holds whatever is fate, and
> Over the border the bar.
> Though rank and fierce the mariner
> Sailing the seven seas,
> He prays, as he holds his glass to his eyes,
> Coaxing the Pleiades.
>
> I cannot love them; and I feel your glad
> Chiding from the grave,
> That my all was only worth at all, what
> Joy to you it gave,
> These seven links the *Law* compelled
> For the human chain—
> I cannot love *them*; and *you*, oh,
> Seven-fold months in Flanders slain!
>
> A jungle there, a cave here, bred six
> And a million years,
> Sure and strong, mate for mate, such
> Love as culture fears;
> I gave you clear the oil and wine;
> You saved me your hob and hearth—
> See how *even* life may be ere the
> Sickle comes and leaves a swath.
>
> But I can wait the seven of moons,
> Or years I spare,
> Hoarding the heart's plenty, nor spend
> A drop, nor share—
> So long but outlives a smile and
> A silken gown;
> Then gayly reach up from my shroud,
> And you, glory-clad, reach down.

In her monologue the widowed wife-woman laments the death of her soldier husband, and cannot console herself with the fact that part of her dead mate survives in their children. A superstitious woman, she is—as are most of Anne Spencer's feminine personae—defiant of cultural mores and societal laws. Shifting from a kind of paganism in the first stanza of the poem to an orthodox religious expression in the poem's conclusion, the wife-woman begins her monologue by praying to the "Maker-of-Sevens." The superstitious wife-woman defines her life in terms of seven—chance and fate—and underscores the idea that most people have the need to pray to some spiritual power. The first line, "Maker-of-Sevens in the scheme of things," may apply to both the wife-woman and the power to which she prays. The wife-woman, as does the "rank and fierce" mariner "Sailing the seven seas," prays to a spiritual force (perhaps the same) which controls the universe—"the scheme of things/From earth to star"—which controls "fate" in this "cycle" of life.

The reference to the "rank and fierce" mariner praying to the Pleiades becomes a more obvious analogy for the entire poem when in the second stanza the wife-woman begins her dramatic prayer for reunion with her dead husband (the motif culminates with the poem's conclusion). She is just as distraught about the loss of her husband as the mariner is about being lost at sea. The central theme of the poem is introduced clearly in the first line of stanza two: the wife-woman's unwillingness and inability to divide her capacity to love into wifely love and motherly love. She cannot love her children ("them") and thus feels her husband's "glad/Chiding from the grave." She still will defy cultural mores and give her all to her mate. She rejects "the *Law*" of nature (biblical doctrine) according to man that says go forth and multiply, the law which "compelled" the "seven links" for the perpetuation of the "human chain" of being. It is a similar cultural tradition of man which was responsible for her husband's military death in Flanders seven months before.

The continuity between the second and third stanzas becomes very intricate as the poem progresses. Moving from pure superstition or paganism in the first stanza to civilization in the second stanza, the poem shows that it is not a pagan but a Christian culture which has created the speaker's problems. Christian civilization and culture "compelled" the "seven links" and thus threatened or took something away from the couple's mate-to-mate love bond. It is also not paganism, but civilization—war— which has deprived the wife-woman of her mate. Stanza three alludes again to the pagan and stresses a positive contrast with the very remote past, before culture or civilization as we now know it. "A jungle there, a cave here" perhaps refers first to the jungle nature of war, the savagery, in modern terms, which has taken her husband's life and left her in despair. "A jungle there, a cave here, bred six/And a million years" in terms of sexual imagery underscores the intensity of the woman's love for her mate. She loved as a savage woman, "Sure and strong, mate for mate," the kind of love thought barbarian by modern civilization for it is "such/Love as culture fears." In the second half of stanza three, Anne Spencer returns to biblical imagery, for the most part, to express again the intensity of wifely love: "I gave you clear the oil and wine." The line suggests if not the Bible, at least that period in history usually associated with it: life at the dawn of western civilization as we know it where the woman's role was to cater to the needs and desires of her husband. The sixth line of this stanza in its language and image provides an imagistic balance between past and present expressions of this kind of wifely love: "You saved me your hob and hearth" (fireplaces, symbols of western civilization's cultural domesticity and felicity). The two lines which close the stanza continue the technique of comparison-contrast. Though the lines allude to several of the poem's different motifs, their main emphasis is on the duality of a domestic love relationship, the sharing of love between wife and husband, "mate for mate," to the exclusion of all others.

The fourth and last stanza reiterates the wife-woman's unwavering position and states that her love is an undying love (what culture may even call selfish). She will "hoard" all her love and wait until the two shall meet again. A poem which began with pagan allusions and overtones now ends with a particularly Christian (or biblical) motif: she will wait until death, "Then gayly reach up from my shroud,/And you, glory-clad, reach down."

It is such an unconventional approach as this in "The Wife-Woman" to what otherwise would be a typical treatment of traditional themes which adds to the interest of Anne Spencer as a poet. Indeed, some of her poems follow so closely traditional techniques and themes that they do little to distinguish her as a poet who had promise or as one of achievement. "The Wife-Woman," I believe, is one of her better achievements. Consistently Anne Spencer has balanced opposites: the pagan and the orthodox religions; the cultural and the uncivilized; wifely love and motherly love. The first half of the poem is contrasted and balanced with the second half; stanza with stanza; line with line. Even the alternating rhyme of the poem does not call attention to itself and functions well in the poem.

Anne Spencer was quick to point out that she was not the wife-woman. She said that members of her family had read relatively few of her poems, but that of those they had read they at times misinterpreted what seemed to be very personal allusions. "The Wife-Woman," some members of her family thought, described Mrs. Spencer's feelings toward her husband and children. This is far from the case. "The wife-woman is not me," she maintained, "she is a poetic character."

At the end of "The Wife-Woman" the speaker looks forward to that death which will reunite her spiritually with her husband. Death was a recurrent theme in Anne Spencer's life and is quite prominent in her writings. In the early part of this chapter I stated that a large portion of the canon of her poetry can be viewed as forming a poetic *Pilgrim's Progress* which concentrates on the quest to escape this world of Vanity Fair and reach an ideal and visionary world of supernal beauty, peace, and harmony. Death is the means by which one achieves this spiritual quest, for one must die a human death and be reborn into a spiritual life (in spite of worldly obstacles) in order to reach the Celestial City of "immortal completeness." Therefore, the desire to transcend this human world of stark reality, sin, and evil and to reach that world of spiritual perfection is what one may arbitrarily term a pursuit of death, a term which I think succinctly describes important overtones in her life and a dominant theme in her writings. The pursuit of death is closely linked with a quest for immortality, and it is these two themes that I will use to divide the following discussion of the remaining poems in that group which coalesce to form a poetic *Pilgrim's Progress*.

Anne Spencer was ill on many occasions during her ninety-three years, and there were times that it seemed she was at the point of death. She probably never feared death, for death was just a means of entering a more beautiful life. Her daughter Bethel told a humorous anecdote about one of her mother's "close calls" with death. There were times when Anne Spencer just wanted to be alone, not to be bothered by human contact. Bethel remembered one occasion long ago—probably not the only one—when Mrs. Spencer was thought seriously ill. She took to her bed, thinking that now she would be left alone. Neighbors and friends sincerely concerned with her health flocked to her bedside. Looking at her lying there so helplessly in the bed, they offered phrases of pity, and Anne Spencer put on an act to feed this pity. While they were looking at or sitting with her—probably not with her permission—she would clutch at the covers as if she were taking her last breath. This frightened the onlookers, and they feared that Mrs. Spencer would not be with them long. After she had rested as long as she desired and had had the solitude she wished, she emerged from the sick bed a well woman. Some years later she evidently told how some of her "attacks" of serious illness were just excuses to be left alone.

Though she feigned serious illness perhaps more than once to gain her seclusion, there were times when she actually was ill and thought she was going to die. Though her life was relatively free of *extended* physical infirmities before 1973, periodically she was seriously ill and often anticipated death. This is evident in her writings as well as in her letters to various people. In several letters to James Weldon Johnson between 1919 and 1937, she often spoke of imminent death. In 1920, for example, about a year after first meeting Johnson, she wrote about an operation she was to undergo, and concluded: "Hold my hands. We who are about to die salute you! . . . I have been ill in bed these last three weeks, and ill out of bed more of them. . . . If Ed sends you my Bible that I've read since I was a girl, it shall mean that you are not to sorrow as one having no hope."[4] Other members of the family seem also to have been plagued by serious illness during this time. In the same letter she wrote: "For some reason my family history of last winter desires to repeat itself." This was perhaps during the winter of 1919 when Edward was very ill with pneumonia.

The subjects of pain, suffering, and death that touched her personal life also are treated in her poetry. She found much beauty amid the "strife" of this human life, but she longed for that peace and joy that would come after death. Life's pains, sufferings, and trials, whether physical, social, or psychological, ultimately were to Anne Spencer kinds of intimations of immortality. In 1924 she wrote to Johnson:

I have not written before because, lately, all my stars surely combined to make me immensely unhappy. . . . I speak this little Jeremiad to you before you come and have done with all lamenting:

> Lord, still I am too strong;
>   All Thy buffets fail,
> But if I abstain long,
>   Willst Thou make me frail?
>
> If I love but lose,
>   If I laugh . . . but cry
> Full my deeper cruse,
>   Willst Thou let me die?[5]

4. Anne Spencer to James Weldon Johnson, January 19, 1920, in James Weldon Johnson Memorial Collection of Negro Arts and Letters, Collection of American Literature, Beinecke Rare Book and Manuscript Library, Yale University.
5. Anne Spencer to James Weldon Johnson, May 8, 1924. The poem was later revised; the revised version is included in the Appendix.

The poem is a death plea in which the speaker laments that she, though ill, is still physically too strong to die. (Mrs. Spencer said that when she wrote this poem she did not literally want to die, or want anyone else to die. As late as July, 1974, she revised the poem in order to delete this direct reference to death.) The speaker asks that if she pretends to want to live, will the Lord then grant the opposite of her wish and allow her to die. The second stanza uses the mask motif, often found in black literature —especially in poetry—with a slight variation. Anne Spencer said that in writing the second stanza she was reminded of a time when she was on her way to work and passed a group of black men doing some menial job characteristic of the low place they had been assigned in society. Yet these men were not openly distressed about their state. One passing by would even think them happy about their lot in life. "A white man passing would look and say, 'ain't niggers jolly,'" Mrs. Spencer said. The men were laughing and joking to keep from crying, she said. In other words, these black men were wearing the psychological racial mask: openly pretending to be one thing when actually they were another. Using a variation of this idea, the speaker of the poem asks the Lord that if she "love but lose" (pretends to accept what she actually rejects), if she "laugh . . . but cry/Full my deeper cruse" (pretends to be happy in this unhappy life), will the Lord then grant her death.

The racial implication which underlies the second stanza of this poem is not readily apparent without Anne Spencer's specific remark that there is such an allusion; but the poem does not depend on this reference for its meaning. Among her papers this is one in a group of three poems titled "Lord Songs," which she later titled "Earth Songs." In the other two poems one can see even larger racial implications. The five-line poem titled "Liability" is the second of the group and has suffering rather than death as its major theme:

> Lord, Thy stripes for me,
> For him the smoothéd pillow;
> My eyes were clear

> To see Thy golden stair,—
> Be mine the willow.

To force a racial connotation on the poem might be to misjudge it. But few of Anne Spencer's poems are overtly about race. And those several poems which can be interpreted as such have a much larger range of meaning: the suffering of a generation, small group, or individual is expanded to include the suffering of a people.

The third poem in the group, "Failure," like the first one, more personally expresses the pursuit of death. Yet its meaning, too, can apply to a larger constituency:

> Master, the harp is broken,
>   Let me die;
> Broken on a sobbing chord,
> Riven by a single word,
> Word by angels never spoken—
>   Master, let me die.

The harp in the poem symbolizes beauty and harmony, and its broken state leads the speaker to desire to leave this world of pain, sorrow, and chaos for the world of peace and harmony to which death will take her. The harp is also a symbol of the poet, whose job it is to bring beauty and harmony into this world. Could it be that this poem was written at a time when Anne Spencer felt her poetic efforts were fruitless, such a time as she would write that all her muses were dead? If so, it may well be an expression of her failure to achieve in her poetry that beauty which she so desired to create in a world of ugliness, a plea to the "Master" to quell that desire which she could not articulate poetically.

The poet's role as a harbinger of spiritual beauty in a carnival wasteland is arduous because in this human world ugliness dims even further the fragile glimmers of beauty; the human overshadows the divine. If we can read "Failure" as an expression of the inability of the poet to create supernal beauty in this world and thus a desire to die into that life where perfect beauty reigns, then the title of the poem seems significant indeed. It is a thwarted quest for beauty and a pursuit of death. The poem "Questing" emphasizes this idea more thoroughly:

> Let me learn now where Beauty is;
> My day is spent too far toward night
> To wander aimlessly and miss her place;
> To grope, eyes shut, and fingers touching space.

In these opening lines the speaker states what the quest is. The symbols of beauty are here on this earth, but the complete and perfect beauty is in a world elsewhere. The poet-speaker has seen the symbols of beauty, the "handmaidens to the Queen," but wants to see the "Queen" herself. As a poet in pursuit of beauty, the speaker is little more than one of the handmaidens. She must continue the quest, though it is probable that in a human life she never can attain that queenly perfection of beauty:

> But let me learn now where Beauty is;
> I was born to know her mysteries,
> And needing wisdom I must go in vain:
> Being sworn bring to some hither land,
> Leaf from her brow, light from her torchéd hand.

As a poet in this world the speaker must strive, "Being sworn," to illuminate the attributes of beauty (the "Leaf" and "light"), but only in death and immortality can this perfect beauty be comprehended.

"Questing" exhibits at least a tinge of anxiety, perhaps a result of the anxiety Anne Spencer felt from the incident which occasioned the poem's composition: her son's elopement and marriage to a lady whom Mrs. Spencer did not like. The poem is in no obvious way about that marriage, but it does attest to what Mrs. Spencer referred to as her method of composition. Often the germinal idea for a poem would be in her mind for days or as long as years before some incident, at times seemingly unrelated to the finished poem, would occur to concretize and give poetic form to the thought. Such was the case with the composition of "Questing."

The general background of the poem involves Anne Spencer's view of the world as a wasteland in which one easily can be enticed from a pursuit of the beautiful. It is not that she desired to infringe upon her son's freedom to determine his personal life (individual freedom was too precious to Anne Spencer for that kind of reaction), or that her reaction was based merely on her dislike for the young lady, but in this particular relationship she sensed a pursuit of the not-beautiful, another of those superficial and fleeting human obstacles placed in the path of one's quest for spiritual perfection. She sensed something not quite sacred in the relationship, and within a few years the marriage ended in divorce. "As soon as I heard Chauncey had eloped with that girl, 'Questing' wrote itself," Mrs. Spencer recalled. She wrote to Johnson a few years after "Questing" was published that it was "praps using to point out D-O-N-T"; that is, don't be too easily entrapped by fake glimmers of beauty and of perfection in a relationship.

The yearning for beauty and perfection through a pursuit of death evolves into a poetic quest for immortality. A firm believer in immortality, Anne Spencer voices this death-to-immortality motif in at least two different ways in her poetry. The first and most obvious expression of this is in "Requiem," where the poet seems to embrace a pantheistic philosophy in which "The grave restores what finds its bed." The poem parallels an idea in Emerson's "Hamatreya," that one cannot own the land but instead is consumed by it. Death in "Requiem" is seen as a natural process of nature where nothing is destroyed but is recycled.

The poem is stated somewhat matter-of-factly in terms of landscape imagery, which carries the same meaning as this imagery does in her other poems. That "far country" of immortality is more than just a beautiful, harmonious place, for there true love reigns eternally. That the objective of true love is "immortal completeness" is the motif which ends "Life-Long, Poor Browning," "Substitution," and "The Wife-Woman"; the same idea is present in other of her poems. Such a poetic attitude toward love for the most part derived from the very special and sacred relationship Mrs. Spencer had with her husband and with a few lifelong friends. After she passed ninety years of age she frequently stated that "a hundred years is long enough to live," and she yearned for death to reunite her with Edward, though she felt that his spiritual influence was ever present at 1313 Pierce Street.

Anne Spencer said that her husband Edward was father, husband, lover, and, most of all, friend. An influential force in her life, he appears often in her poetry. In her poems one sees fathers; more frequently one sees husbands, lovers, and friends, and at times the three are not differentiated. In "Translation" the journey of the two people into the "far country" is the journey of "My friend and I." In the middle of the poem we see the "wooing Kestrel" who "mutes his mating note" and the reference to love and lovers begins to emerge. By the end of the poem the friend merges with the lover. At this point the couple have reached the zenith of their relationship, and in this eternal "far country" the spirit of the divine hovers over them and brings them peace from the "anvil and strife" characteristic of the world they left: "And the air fleeced its particles for a coverlet;/When star after star came out/To guard their lovers in oblivion." That this "far country" is a spiritual place of divine qualities, that the entire poem recalls again Anne Spencer's recurring themes of the pursuit of death and the quest for immortality is suggested in the middle of the poem with the notation of the *time* of this journey—"at day's end."

Many of the "friends" in Anne Spencer's poems are references to people other than Edward Spencer. Commenting on the sacredness of friendship, she said, "There are two things that happen to *real* friends. Of a *real* friend you don't ask a lot of questions. And if he dies, you still have that friend's influence on you." The comments were made in reference to the second half of her poem "I Have a Friend":

> He does not ask me how beloved
> Are my husband and children,
> Nor ever do I require
> Details of life and love

In the grave—his home,—
We are such friends.

"Translation" contains a similar idea: "Our deeper content
was never spoken,/But each knew all the other said." Mrs.
Spencer explained that she used the present tense "have" because once one has a friend, that friend remains throughout
eternity. Of the several entries in her Notebooks concerning
friendship, one notation in particular perhaps states concisely
her attitude toward the subject: "Friendship is such a tenuous
thing it must be strong and deathless to exist at all." Friendship
is not one of the weaknesses of "mere humanity" ("Letter to My
Sister"), but is spiritual and lasts forever. This kind of friendship
describes her association with James Weldon Johnson, and if "I
Have a Friend" had been written after Johnson's death, one
would tend to think that the poem was a reference to him. The
husband-lover-friend in her poems is often associated with the
symbol of perfection, spiritual beauty, and all that is sacred: the
garden. In this connection her poem to Johnson, "For Jim, Easter
Eve," comes to the forefront. That she held Johnson in this light
was clear not only in her conversations about him but also in her
letters to him where she frequently addressed him as "Gem."

Mrs. Spencer said that she had met but few people in her life
whom she would classify with "Gem." Elsie Brown, her childhood playmate in Bramwell, West Virginia, her husband Edward, Bernice Lomax Hill, and possibly Langston Hughes are
among the few. Her special meaning of friendship implies a
spiritual communion and is different from, though not necessarily superior or inferior to, the love one has for one's family
and acquaintances. She loved people in general, and said that
she would have had little trouble getting along with her enemies
or with those who might have hated her. Her special friends
were few, and she met few people in her life whom she thoroughly detested. An interesting notation on the subject in her
Notebooks reads: "Small wonder we hate our enemies. If we
could bring loved ones back to life, we'd kill 'em, completely,

two or three times a year." Her basic attitude toward friendship is typified by the following entry from her Notebooks:

Worthwhile things not only must have a standard measurement while we live, but the [trial] of their truth is found in death. Considering—taking for instance the first worthwhile unit, Time conservation—we find the arresting thought that we *spend* time to buy *eternity*. Surely a thought readily understood in so commercial a generation as our own. We must spend time in solving the human equation—with our ears close to the heart of life, listening and eager to serve; in advocating a new day in service to one another—the existence of a normality so fine that "Serve Ye, one another" shall be the very correct paraphrase for "Love Ye," that our bit may be done to widen the narrow perspectives of the server and the served. Wightman's lines entitled servants are expressive. Again, we should spend our time for friendship; not to seek friends, nor cajole them nor try to hold them lest they run away—such methods dishonor friendship.

When the major themes of her poems coalesce—a rejection of deceptive earthly symbols of perfection and beauty, a rejection of sin and evil, a pursuit of death, and a quest for immortality—it follows that the pilgrimage, a journey as well as a quest, would emerge as a recurrent motif. The personae of her poems often are presented as pilgrims rejecting this fleeting life in search of the Celestial City of infinite beauty and good, both thematically and dramatically.

This interpretation of a large group of her poems as forming a poetic or aesthetic *Pilgrim's Progress* is arbitrary, for it is doubtful that Anne Spencer consciously intended a particular thematic or philosophical design for her poems as a whole. If such an interpretation is plausible, what it shows, then, is that indeed Anne Spencer was that "private poet" which she had been called; that this design flowed naturally from her pen; and that her poetry, a private record of her attitude toward life, mirrors in poetic form the ideas and themes which shaped her life and personality. Moreover, since her poetry may not adhere absolutely to this analogous interpretation, what it shows, then, is that not only did Anne Spencer not consciously design her poems to fit such a philosophic scheme, but that since this was private poetry, she was not concerned to any large degree with the publication of her poems.

8 ❧ The Poetry: Controversy

During their literary careers most black writers have, in varying degrees, dealt with racial themes. Though the canon of Anne Spencer's poetry is not racially oriented, this does not mean that she was not concerned with racial problems. Yet one may wonder why Anne Spencer, a woman who always voiced a deep concern with the race question, a woman who was fully aware of and proud of her blackness, and a woman who for decades was actively involved in destroying racial barriers, avoided racial themes in most of her poetry. Her poems reflect something that is more intimate and personal than skin color or ethnic origin. In addition to her statement that she did not love and hate by color, race, or ethnic origin, she perhaps answered this question best in the headnote she wrote to her poems in Countee Cullen's *Caroling Dusk*: "I write about some of the things I love. But have no civilized articulation for the things I hate."[1] Writing briefly and succinctly about herself, she included in the headnote:

Mother Nature, February, forty-five years ago forced me on the stage that I, in turn, might assume the role of lonely child, happy wife, perplexed mother—and, so far, a twice resentful grandmother. I have no academic honors, nor lodge regalia. I am a Christian by intention, a Methodist by inheritance, and a Baptist by marriage. . . . I proudly love being a Negro woman—[it's] so involved and interesting. *We* are the PROBLEM—the great national game of TABOO.

Though she avoided an excess of topical and controversial themes in her poetry, it would seem from references in her let-

1. Quoted in Countee Cullen (ed.), *Caroling Dusk: An Anthology of Verse by Negro Poets* (New York: Harper, 1927), 47.

ters that the prose she wrote was topical and controversial. The article which was rejected was a political one and the story or stories and the novel mentioned in her letters concerned politics or race. Her inability to write about the things for which she had "no civilized articulation" might have affected the quality of the prose pieces she wrote, and in part might have accounted for their rejection. Her failure to write primarily or unmistakably about being black in America is perhaps one reason her works have not received the attention they deserve.

The discussion of her poetry in Chapter 7 primarily involves the correlation between the private person and the private poet of aestheticism. The poems which form another group (and which span more than a forty-year period) share the general theme of human freedom and disclose affinities between Anne Spencer the social heretic and Anne Spencer the poet of contumacy. The poems in this group are at times topical, at times controversial—advocating racial and ethnic sovereignty, feminist rights, and individual liberties. Individual poems in this group have more than occasional thematic affinities to the typical racial protest poems of this century, but Anne Spencer is cautious enough to treat her material in a manner which allows the poems to transcend topicality, and thus she gives a broader scope to what otherwise would be dated poems of much less substance and effectiveness. For example, "White Things" is certainly a topical poem. But the approach the poet takes to her subject matter distinguishes it thematically and technically from the majority of racial protest poems of the time (1920s)—and perhaps most such poems written before and after this, many of which are included in anthologies more, I suspect, because of the general reputation of their authors and the social and literary history of the times than for the total and timeless effectiveness of the poems themselves. In most of the poems in the "freedom" group Anne Spencer uses specificity of action and incident in a way which does not confine any one poem to a particular time, place, or dated ideology.

"I almost wrote 'White Things' several times," said Anne

Spencer when referring to some racial incident or situation which infuriated her. But what caused her to put the poem on paper was her reading in Monroe Work's *Negro Year Book* the account of a pregnant black woman who was seized by a lynch mob and cut through the abdomen to kill her and her unborn child. The incident to which she referred probably was the one reported in Work's *Negro Year Book* for 1918[2] (which gives a clue to the approximate date "White Things" was composed). Work mentions the lynching, but does not record the specific details Mrs. Spencer recounted to me. Though the story was reported by several journalists in many publications, it just might be that she read Walter White's account of this same lynching, published in *Thirty Years of Lynching in the United States* (1919):

Georgia, 1918

Hampton Smith, a white farmer, had the reputation of ill treating his Negro employees. Among those whom he abused was Sidney Johnson, a Negro peon, whose fine of thirty dollars he had paid when he was up before the court for gaming. After having been beaten and abused, the Negro shot and killed Smith as he sat in his window at home. He also shot and wounded Smith's wife.

For this murder a mob of white men of Georgia for a week, May 17 to 24, engaged in a hunt for the guilty man, and in the meantime lynched the following innocent persons: Will Head, Will Thompson, Hayes Turner, Mary Turner, his wife, for loudly proclaiming her husband's innocence, Chime Riley and four unidentified Negroes. Mary Turner was pregnant and was hung by her feet. Gasoline was thrown on her clothing and it was set on fire. Her body was cut open and her infant fell to the ground with a little cry, to be crushed to death by the heel of one of the white men present. The mother's body was then riddled with bullets. The murderer, Sidney Johnson, was at length located in a house in Valdosta.

The house was surrounded by a posse headed by the Chief of Police and Johnson, who was known to be armed, fired until his shot gave out, wounding the Chief. The house was entered and Johnson found dead. His body was mutilated. After the lynching more than 500 Ne-

2. Monroe N. Work (ed.), *Negro Year Book: An Encyclopedia of the Negro, 1917–1918* (Tuskegee Institute, Ala.: Negro Year Book Publishing Co., 1919), 74.

groes left the vicinity of Valdosta, leaving hundreds of acres of untilled land behind them.[3]

White's account corresponds in detail here to what Mrs. Spencer told me about the incident which precipitated "White Things."

The poem follows her usual structural scheme, but in reverse; it moves from a quiet, positive tone to one of defiance and determination, climaxing in a powerful statement of its theme. She uses the traditional connotations of white and black (good and evil, positive and negative), only to reverse these connotations through imagery and language and thus retrieve the poem from that category of so many racial protest poems which are rendered ineffective as time passes either because of their racial romanticism (melodramatic laments about the plight of blacks in America or sentimental longings for a remote African past) or because such poems are mere rhetoric clothed in seemingly contrived tones of anger and indignation. A finely executed protest poem, and perhaps one of her best poems, "White Things" closely interweaves natural scenery with motifs of freedom and human frailties, with religious overtones.

> Most things are colorful things—the sky, earth, and sea.
>   Black men are most men; but the white are free!
> White things are rare things; so rare, so rare
> They stole from out a silvered world—somewhere.
> Finding earth-plains fair plains, save greenly grassed,
> They strewed white feathers of cowardice, as they passed;
>   The golden stars with lances fine
>   The hills all red and darkened pine,
> They blanched with their wand of power;
> And turned the blood in a ruby rose
> To a poor white poppy-flower.
>
> They pyred a race of black, black men,
> And burned them to ashes white; then,

3. *Thirty Years of Lynchings in the United States, 1889–1918* (New York: NAACP, 1919), 26–27. The account here seems to be taken from a much fuller one written by Walter White, *The Lynchings of May, 1918, in Brooks and Lowndes Counties, Georgia,* and published by the National Association for the Advancement of Colored People.

> Laughing, a young one claimed a skull,
> For the skull of a black is white, not dull,
> But a glistening awful thing;
> Made, it seems, for this ghoul to swing
> In the face of God with all his might,
> And swear by the hell that siréd him:
> "Man-maker, make white!"

One of the basic statements of the poem comes in the second line: "Black men are most men; but the white are free!" The first stanza proposes through images of natural scenery that white men have erected a human hierarchy based on whiteness. Perhaps alluding remotely to Scandinavian military history and the conquest of western European nations, and referring more specifically to the spread of western European civilization in the Americas, the poem's first stanza asserts that whites "stole from out a silvered world—somewhere" on their imperialistic quest, and "Finding earth-plains fair plains, save greenly grassed, / They strewed white feathers of cowardice, as they passed." Their violation of nature prefaced their destructive campaign to subjugate human nature and deprive other men of the human right to be free. Continually narrowing its scope from the general (black men referring to the dark-skinned peoples of the world) to the more specific (black Americans), the poem does not limit its reference in the first stanza to the dominance of white over black, but through color imagery includes the red man among the "colorful things," and, therefore, begins to develop more specific implications for American civilization.

The fundamental analogy in the first stanza is one between nature and men of color. Both have been violated and subjugated by white men's "lances fine." With a maniacal drive to wield power and spread whiteness, white men have blanched "The hills all red and darkened pine . . . / And turned the blood in a ruby rose / To a poor white poppy-flower."

The structural device of general to particular shows a careful balance and transition between the two stanzas, the metaphors and images easily and smoothly giving way to the more specific message of the poem, unveiled in the second stanza. Stanza two decries the white race's hostility in America toward the black race. The old phrase "the only good nigger is a dead nigger" (a slight modification of the phrase used for the red man) is dramatized in this stanza, because only after the black man's destruction does the white man see him in any favorable light. After the lynching, after the burning, "Laughing, a young one claimed a skull, / For the skull of a black is white, not dull, / But a glistening awful thing." The claiming of the skull recalls the practice of whites collecting souvenirs from their victims during the usually festive atmosphere of a lynching scene. At the same time the lines suggest the likeness of men ("For the skull of a black man is white, not dull") in that all men are men and are basically alike in the eyes of God. Important is the irony in this stanza: the "ghoul" is attracted to his victim only after the victim's blackness has been "pyred" into "ashes white." The overwhelming paradox of the first lines of this stanza (and in the poem as a whole) is that to destroy the symbol of the black man's spirituality, his color, is to destroy his essence. The objective of whiteness is to reign supreme, and necessarily subjugate or destroy all in its path.

The concluding four lines of the poem take a sharp twist and reverse the universal connotations of black and white, for the young white man who "claimed" the skull is the "ghoul." And though he is attracted only to the whiteness of the skull, at this point white itself is negative. The lines suggest that the psychological sustenance for whites is in destroying blackness. The last four lines, which contain the essential meaning for the entire poem, must be read together to grasp the continuity of their meaning.

The concerns of the two stanzas culminate in the last four lines. In the first stanza the white man has tried to dominate nature—both physical objects and human beings. God is nature, and in trying to control nature the white man has endeavored to control God, which the concluding lines of the second stanza reiterate. Destruction of the black man is a destruction of God's works, and in doing so the white man with his "wand of power" had defied God and damned the majority of His creations— "colorful things." In his obsession with whiteness the white man in essence had demanded: "Man-maker, make white"; that is, that white things be the only things of worth in this world.

Richard Wright is one of the very few writers who have handled this particular theme of racial protest—*whiteness*—as perceptively as Anne Spencer has in "White Things." In the first half of *Black Boy* (1945) Wright presents a similar conception of the phenomenon of whiteness. In American culture, especially but not exclusively that of the South, Wright sees whiteness as an almost cosmic force regulating the lives of black people. Wright ultimately asserts that whiteness is absolute authority; that it is "a culture, a creed, a religion" [4] by which men's lives, black and white, are determined and regulated. In both Wright's book and Anne Spencer's poem there is an acknowledged difference between the cosmic force of God and the all-powerful force of whiteness. Both authors show that the distinction is somewhat out of order, that God's cosmic force has been so undermined and perverted by humans that it is subject to the dictates of whiteness. Neither writer emphasizes white people as individuals, but both show that this concept of whiteness is so deeply rooted in the American mind and culture that it transcends mere human and individual control. It is revealed as a power which in one way or another writes and administers our laws, regulates our personal and public lives, interprets our religion, and rules our civilization. Americans have made whiteness the quintessence of Americanism.

Though one must be careful not to force racial interpretations on certain of her poems, many of them (for example, two of the "Earth Songs") do operate on more than one level and contain racial allusions and connotations. Such a poem is "Grapes: Still-Life." It is not just about grapes. If one chooses to assign racial connotations, then the "globes" are the men of color, that ma-

4. Richard Wright, *Black Boy: A Record of Childhood and Youth* (New York: Harper, 1945), 65.

jority of the world's human population traced back to the origin of man. They are the "Aged essence of the sun." A comparison between the history of grape culture in America (and in the world) and the history of blacks in America (and their relations with other races here) might show definite racial affinities on which this poem is based. The cultivation of grapes can be traced to the earliest recorded history of man. The old world (European) and new world (American) grape culture; the varieties of grapes native to America; the various regional and sectional grape cultures; the grafting and crossbreeding of grapes; the physical and visual characteristics of the varieties of grapes, and so forth; all these aspects of grape culture in America are implicit in the metaphorical correlation of grapes and men. It is the last stanza of the poem—which may be a somewhat too obvious moral tag—which suggests this metaphorical parallel. The poem as a whole is thus another example of Anne Spencer's use of the "familiar," that poetic method stated in "1975."

"The Sévignés," a poem about the "peculiar institution" of American slavery and its effects, is based on an analogy, and demonstrates again how she could "make a poem" from her reading and associating ideas. In 1930 she was reading an article titled "Louisiana, Land of Perpetual Romance" in *National Geographic Magazine*. The article included the picture of a statue of an "Old-Time Darkey" recently erected in a public square in Natchitoches, Louisiana. The caption under the picture of the statue reads:

It is peculiarly significant that in this Louisiana town, where one group of historians has vigorously promoted the claim that on a plantation near here were enacted scenes upon which the closing tragic episode of "Uncle Tom's Cabin" were based, and another group of investigators, with equal vigor, has descried [*sic*] such an association, that should be erected this unique statue.[5]

This picture and the content of the article so affected her that she

5. "Louisiana, Land of Perpetual Romance," *National Geographic Magazine*, LVII (January, 1930), 393–482.

sketched a very rough draft of a poem which since then she greatly improved and titled "The Sévignés."

The title of the poem comes from the connection Mrs. Spencer saw between the subject of her poem and the letters of a noted seventeenth-century French aristocrat, Madame Marie de Rabutin Chantal, Marquise de Sévigné (1626–1696). Anne Spencer many times spoke sarcastically about the "American Sévignés" and referred specifically, in reference to this poem, to letters of Madame de Sévigné which reveal her to be preoccupied with the gossip of her social class and insensitive to the plight of the lower classes. "It has shocked Madame de Sévigné's readers to see with what complaisance she wrote of these wretched people's sufferings." [6]

Even more important for the background of "The Sévignés" is that Madame de Sévigné's attitude toward the French peasants was the norm rather than the exception for her aristocratic circle and for France's aristocracy in general during this period.

> The seventeenth century in France was . . . a time of high civilisation; but it was also a brutal time. Men were hard, cruel and unscrupulous. . . . These cultured aristocrats, these elegant ladies—who were reduced to tears by Racine's pathos, who admired Poussin and Claude, who crowded to listen to the sermons of Bourdaloue and Massillon, who were so delicately sensitive to the sadness and beauty of the country—looked upon the peasants as hardly human. They used them as they would never have used their horses or their dogs. Madame de Sévigné shared the common opinions of her day. [7]

The objective of Anne Spencer's poem, and thus the direct meaning of its title, is to draw a parallel between "These cultured aristocrats" in seventeenth-century France and those Europeans who immigrated to what became the United States (especially the French immigrants who settled in Louisiana) and who eventually established a cultural aristocracy with class dis-

6. William Somerset Maughm, "Preface" to Violet Hammersley (trans. and ed.), *Letters from Madame la Marquise de Sévigné* (London: Secker and Warburg, 1955), 18.
7. *Ibid.*, 18–19.

tinctions (based on race and slavery) similar to those in the France of Madame de Sévigné's day. The last line of the poem conveys this, and states even further that the cultured aristocracy of America was composed of that same class of pariahs who emigrated from France. The poem's province is not confined to Natchitoches, Louisiana, but encompasses the entire slaveholding section of the United States and has implications for the race problem in the whole of the American nation.

Contrasting two well-known literary characters, Anne Spencer gives shape to her thoughts. She often said that the twentieth century's connotations of the term *Uncle Tom* had done an injustice to Harriet Beecher Stowe's intentions in creating her title character in *Uncle Tom's Cabin*. As she explained to me in a letter, Uncle Remus is closer to what modern usage terms an Uncle Tom.

Every group has been able to survive a lot of epithets, name-calling, and so on but I think Uncle Tom is the [one put in] situations invariably applied by an ignorant non-reader. For instance, in Eleanor Wilson [Randolph] McAdoo's book, *The Priceless Gift*—possibly [Woodrow] Wilson's daughter—she tells of her father saying when she was a kid returning from a visit to the South that she came back "talking like an educated nigger." If her accent had been that of Dear Darky, I'm sure it would have delighted Woodrow Wilson. So it is through the strength of the *intelligent nigger* we keep the [staunch position?] we've reached. Dear Darky and Uncle Remus were slave falsities. In a book by James Branch Cabell (a liberal) the author says his nurse preferred the whites she nursed to her own brood!

Speaking of the poem at another time she stated: "A *nigger* will smile in a white man's face and at the same time cut his throat. Uncle Remus was wrapped up in his white folks, whereas Uncle Tom was a hero who died for black womanhood. Uncle Remus was a darky; Uncle Tom may have been a nigger." She makes the distinction in her poem between the two characters, for the statue she uses symbolically in the poem is a "shameless thing set up to the intricate involvement of human slavery." The final lines of the poem sound the irony and paradox of the so-called American democracy, for this slave replica is a monument to the "callous" nation of people who "fled from the / slavery of Europe" with the intention of establishing and maintaining human liberties. It is an ironic monument to those very documents of American democracy which were written by men who on the one hand were theoretical heralds of human liberties and on the other hand were simultaneously enslaving the black man and had practically annihilated the red man.[8]

It is regrettable that we do not have more of Anne Spencer's racial protest poems, especially poems as well done as "White Things." But, as a private poet, Anne Spencer did not see racial protest as her métier in poetry. "I write about some of the things I love. But have no civilized articulation for the things I hate," she explained in Cullen's *Caroling Dusk*. These are words which come up again and again when one looks at the poet and her works. We see Anne Spencer as a novelty because a black woman during her time and in her locale wrote a kind of poetry which we say is not "typical." Such an attitude is both positive and negative. This is to say that Anne Spencer as a black American poet is interesting because of the poetry she wrote as well as because of the poetry she did not write, as though one would necessarily expect her to write racial protest poetry. Black American poets many times have been placed in a precarious situation by readers and critics. On the one hand, black American poets, from Phillis Wheatley to Dunbar to Cullen to present-day poets who are black but who are not writing in the "new black poetry" vein, have been damned by critics and readers both black and white because they did not write (or do not write) about "the black experience in America," as if all blacks in America have only one and the same experience. On the other hand, they have been criticized because they did write about the experiences shared by many blacks in America. It is as though the absence or presence of black subject matter in poetry by black American writers is the only important aspect of their poetry. At the turn of the century William Dean Howells all but stated that the only

8. For general information in this area, see Winthrop D. Jordan, *White Over Black: American Attitudes Toward the Negro, 1550–1812* (Chapel Hill: University of North Carolina Press, 1968).

contribution Paul Laurence Dunbar made to American literature was his dialect poetry, specifically that which recorded the dialects of black Americans.[9] The poet-critic Louis Simpson, reviewing Gwendolyn Brooks's *Selected Poems* for *Book Week*, wrote: "I am not sure it is possible for a Negro to write well without making us aware he is a Negro; on the other hand, if being a Negro is the only subject, the writing is not important."[10] I shall not compare Anne Spencer to another poet, but when comparing her different poems, one can see that she writes equally well about racial subjects and nonracial subjects, without making us aware that she is black.

During the Harlem Renaissance years, the period when practically all of her poems were published, racial poetry was at its height, rivaled only by the surge of interest in the 1960s and 1970s. With the exception of Langston Hughes and Claude McKay, most of the black poets of the Harlem period, it seems to me, wrote primarily that kind of racial romanticism and protest poetry which critics and readers looked for and expected, for one reason or another. So why not Anne Spencer? In a letter to James Weldon Johnson she spoke of the type of racial poetry being written and so readily accepted during the 1920s: "I react to life more as a human being than as a Negro being, but I admit the latter is 1927 model. The Tom-Tom *forced* into poetry seems a sad state to me."[11] "The Tom-Tom *forced* into poetry" is an accurate description of a large bulk of poetry produced by the Harlem Renaissance (and even post-Renaissance) writers. Indeed,

9. Howell's criticism of Dunbar may be open to interpretation. The reader should consult Howell's "Introduction" to Paul Laurence Dunbar, *Lyrics of Lowly Life* (1896; New York: Dodd, Mead and Co., 1926), xiii–xx. In a letter to a friend dated March 15, 1897, Dunbar reacted to Howell's evaluation of his dialect and standard English poetry: "I see now very clearly that Mr. Howells has done me irrevocable harm in the dictum he laid down regarding my dialect verse." Quoted in Alain Locke (ed.), *The New Negro* (1925; New York: Antheneum, 1968), 38. Jean Wagner documents his topic well in *Black Poets of the United States from Paul Laurence Dunbar to Langston Hughes*, trans. Kenneth Douglas (Urbana: University of Illinois Press, 1973), 108–109, *passim*.

10. *Book Week*, October 27, 1963, p. 25.

11. Anne Spencer to James Weldon Johnson, undated, in James Weldon Johnson Memorial Collection of Negro Arts and Letters, Collection of American Literature, Beinecke Rare Book and Manuscript Library, Yale University.

the criticism inherent in this phrase may be applied to many literary productions characteristic of this and later periods of American literary history.

One should be careful, however, not to criticize black writers before the 1940s too harshly for what they did and did not publish, for before the 1940s it is plausible that many if not most black writers did not have the freedom to publish what they wished and often had to acquiesce to the tastes of those critics, editors, and publishers who controlled publishing outlets.

Anne Spencer is among those writers of the Harlem Renaissance period who chose to limit their publications rather than conform to the dictates of critics and editors and publishers who prejudged for the readers. Her conflict with H. L. Mencken grew out of this same controversy. Mrs. Spencer said that one reason her publication of race poems was limited at this time was that her friend Alain Locke, influential in the publishing career of several black writers of the 1920s, was occupied with promoting Countee Cullen in preference to her. Mrs. Spencer said that Locke rejected an early and short version of her poem about John Brown because Cullen had prepared a poem on the same topic. Locke also objected to (and edited) portions of "Lady, Lady." Mrs. Spencer further stated that the editors who published "White Things" deleted a stanza (or portion of a stanza?) because of a specific reference to "white men"—a reference, I recall her having said, that was thought untimely and unwise at that time for a new black writer dependent on others for publication. And though she never spoke to me of the approximate number of protest poems she had written, I infer from comments she made that her editors, critics, and friends found the kind of racial protest poem she wrote unacceptable in the 1920s.

Not all of the protest poems she wrote in the 1920s were confined to the subject of racial protest in America. The Terence MacSwiney poem (which she wished to be left untitled) is based on the young Irish hero whose seventy-four-day hunger strike in protest of the continued English domination of Ireland precipitated his death in 1922.[12] It is a good poem, one which sounds those notes of freedom and defiance which were so prominent in Anne Spencer's thoughts. Having completed the poem shortly after MacSwiney's death, she told Edward that she would try to get it published in England: "Pop asked me why I was sending the poem there. I told him that I wanted to get an English reaction—they were fighting the Irish." She recalled that she sent the poem to the Manchester *Guardian*, and though the editor liked the poem, it was rejected. This was the first and only poem she submitted for publication on her own, she said; its rejection caused her to shy away from sending her poems directly to publishers. She remembered the rejection letter praised the poem but then asked why she would ruin a good poem with such a last line ("Now lovers have another name to die by"). "The Manchester *Guardian*," she said, "called the ending foolish because the modern view then was that 'lovers' has no image but sex." Mrs. Spencer maintained that poets do not have to say everything they mean, that she meant "freedom lovers" but did not want to use the adjective in the poem. Since then she worked on the last line, often substituting "Ireland" for "freedom lovers." Finally she decided that she would let it stand as it was first written, for she liked the line, though others might object to it.

It is not surprising that Anne Spencer would be attracted to Terence MacSwiney more for his revolutionary ideas and character than for his modest literary output. Such persons as John Brown, Terence MacSwiney, LeRoi Jones (Imamu Baraka), among several others—ardent defenders of human rights—appealed to her. And though she said her favorite poet was Robert Browning, it was Olive Schreiner (1855–1920),[13] a person in the John Brown-Terence MacSwiney-LeRoi Jones category, who Mrs. Spencer said most influenced her own life as a

12. For details of his life and death, see P. S. O'Hagarty, *A Short Memoir of Terence MacSwiney* (Dublin: Talbot Press, 1922).
13. See Vera Buchanan-Gould, *Not Without Laughter: The Life and Writings of Olive Schreiner* (London: Hutchinson & Co., 1949).

private citizen and as a poet. Mrs. Spencer was first introduced to the writings of Olive Schreiner about 1900, when Edward sent her a copy of one of Mrs. Schreiner's books (perhaps *The Story of an African Farm*, 1883, or *Dream Life and Real Life*, 1893). This was when young Edward was working as a porter on a train route between New York and Montreal, and, knowing how much Annie loved books, he sent her as many books as he could while he was working out of New York. Olive Schreiner's book was right for young Annie's mind—more so than the novels of Laura Jean Libbey, Horatio Alger, and other similar writers whom she had been reading for years—and after reading it she then read as much as she could acquire thereafter by and about Mrs. Schreiner.

"The sketch of Olive Schreiner in *Twentieth Century Authors* is so one with me," Mrs. Spencer pointed out. A South African novelist and essayist, Olive Emilie Albertina Schreiner was largely self-educated through her "passionate" reading habit. She was "a severe self-disciplinarian" and became a "Free Thinker" early in life—and as a consequence was alienated from nearly all of her family. Mrs. Schreiner "seems to have been almost born a Rationalist, a feminist, and an extreme liberal in economics and politics." [14]

That Olive Schreiner was outspokenly critical of the way non-white pariahs were treated by the South African establishment, and that she was a radical and a feminist, provided Anne Spencer with a model by which to shape her own life. Anne Spencer was an active and vocal advocate of feminist rights throughout her adult life. She abhorred societal restrictions and discrimination based on sex as vehemently as she detested and defied racial oppression and discrimination. Indeed, the theme of feminine liberation found its way into at least three of her poems: an early poem, "Before the Feast at Shushan"; one during her mid-

14. Stanley J. Kunitz and Howard Haycroft (eds.), *Twentieth Century Authors: A Biographical Dictionary of Modern Literature* (New York: H. H. Wilson Co., 1942), 1247.

dle period of poetic activity, "Po' Little Lib"; and one of her last poems, "The Lemming: O Sweden."

Though her protest poems that deal specifically with the condition of black people in America are very few, she maintained, "Whatever is poetic with me does not belong to poor white folks; it belongs to being Negro." Race is neither an obvious theme in nor motivation for most of her poetry; but Mrs. Spencer maintained that it was this personal racial identity which significantly shaped her view of the world and thus provided for a particular point of view in her writings, regardless of the manifest subject matter. She applied this contention to Robert Browning and his poetry in order to explain why Browning was her favorite poet: "Browning is everything; being Negro, we think alike." (The reference here is to Browning's ancestry. His grandmother, Margaret Tittle, was a West Indian Creole.)

Throughout her life Anne Spencer craved, cherished, and fought for freedom. In her poetry this love of freedom is expressed quite directly at times (as in "Creed": "And all the wild birds this year should know / I cherish their freedom to come and go"); at other times it is more subtly stated. In any case, freedom is a major theme in her life and poetry, and she often directly or indirectly links freedom with the world of nature. In "Before the Feast at Shushan" it is in the Garden of Shushan that Vashti so boldly asserts her independence and her desire for freedom. But the setting here is incidental to the more perspicuous theme of feminism. The poem, based on Book I of Esther in the Old Testament, perhaps attests to the influence of Anne Spencer's avid reading in the Bible since her childhood. According to the biblical story, Ahasuerus is disturbed because of Vashti's actions, actions deviating from the role the Persian society assigned to women in general. The beautiful queen Vashti is sent for and Ahasuerus makes what seems another attempt to quell her ideas of love and her rebellious nature. Though he probably loves Vashti, this love has caused him to yield in ways which subvert his image of self and the image he has in the eyes of his subjects; his concessions thus far have "nearly shamed" him. This is the situation immediately preceding the dramatic action of the poem.

In the poem itself Ahasuerus views Vashti basically as a sex object and attempts to keep this relationship primarily on a physical plane. The problem is that his love on the physical level has been threatened by Vashti's attempts to teach him the "new thing": that a woman is not merely a sex object, that love is more than physical intimacies and should be deemed so by both parties. Ahasuerus must reject this, for to acquiesce would make Vashti, a woman, his peer.

The poem, a reflective monologue by King Ahasuerus, takes place in the garden of the palace of Shushan sometime before the feast, as recorded in the Book of Esther. In the first half of the poem the king wavers somewhat in his attitude toward Vashti and his determination to resist the "new thing." But reflecting on the situation, he maintains that Vashti's actions are most inappropriate for this particular time. It is just before the feast and any deviations from society's sexual roles would seriously damage the king's self-image and compromise his masculinity and authority in the presence of his subjects. At the end of the monologue, therefore, Ahasuerus decides that his roles as king and man must take precedence over any love he feels for Vashti, and, as the last stanza shows, he embraces male chauvinism:

> I, thy Lord, like not manna for meat as a Judahn;
> I, thy master, drink, and red wine, plenty, and when
> I thirst. Eat meat, and full, when I hunger.
> I, thy King, teach you and leave you, when I list.
> No woman in all Persia sets out strange action
> To confuse Persia's lord—
> Love is but desire and thy purpose fulfillment;
> I, thy King, so say!

When one considers "Before the Feast at Shushan" and "The Lemming: O Sweden," one sees again that Anne Spencer is concerned with controversial themes which are not restricted to a particular historical era for their applicability. The motifs of male chauvinism and feminism are evident in "The Lemming: O

Sweden," a poem which deals with another aspect of the general theme of freedom. Mrs. Spencer said that she never quite perfected the poem to her satisfaction, but sent it as is to a friend of hers to show that she "could be modern." Though the poem may not be finished, it still is effective. "The Lemming: O Sweden" is an excerpt from a conversation between a man and a woman over a political question: black soldiers deserting the military and seeking political asylum in Sweden. In the poem proper the man is echoing one of "those good clichés" about the intellectual inferiority of women—in particular, the inability of a woman to understand politics. The first stanza concludes with the idea that "the Eves of this world" are frivolous and selfish, that they look at life as a game and think life is centered on the "I-Me-Mine" equation.

The female speaker in "The Lemming: O Sweden" is similar to Vashti in that she is trying to teach this man the "new thing." The premise of femine intellectual inferiority is dated, the woman retorts in the second stanza:

> She: "For yourself, Sir, you are very old
> academy. No new sense; those good clichés
> when our earth was square, and
> we all fell off the edge . . . "

This stanza suggests that the male speaker, while trying to impose his view on his female companion, unsuccessfully resorts to the argument that since she is a woman she is not expected to understand politics, and evidently is apologizing for even trying to discuss a political topic with her. Basically this is the situation which precedes the poem, and what we get in the first two stanzas is actually a digression from the conversation at hand.

One wonders what definite purpose Anne Spencer had in mind when she allowed the woman in the poem to have the last word. In any case, the final stanza brings us closer to the title and intended theme of the poem. Referring more specifically to the poem's title, the poet uses the metaphor of the suicidal lemming to describe the political situation of black American sol-

diers blindly searching for a better life. There are several sugges-
tive meanings in the last ten-line stanza. On the surface, the
lemming metaphor compares these soldiers' plight to that of the
lemming in that the soldiers were blindly fleeing to a world
which may be (and perhaps is) as deadly as the one which they
left. Perhaps she had in mind reports that black soldiers who
sought political asylum in Sweden found that Sweden was not
free of the racial discrimination characteristic of the United
States. (One notes here that the dark–light imagery in the poem
is used for the same assertion prominent in "White Things": the
western world is caught up in whiteness and blacks will suffer
racial discrimination wherever they go.) The poet also seems
to imply in this stanza a comparison between civilization as we
know it now and the life of the lemming. Periodically the lemming blindly seeks his destruction; and periodically western
civilization through wars seeks its own destruction: "war is so
circle."

The literal meaning of the last stanza is an explanation of the
woman's scar, which she received from one of the lemmings,
apparently part of the topic of conversation before the poem
proper begins. The lemming is a brave and courageous animal
that will not flee when it senses danger but will hiss and bare its
teeth in readiness for defense. This particular lemming was perhaps on its suicidal march because it had lost its protective cov-
ering (one of the reasons, scientists suggest, for the strange and
periodic suicidal march of the lemmings into the sea where they
drown): the arctic "winter had touched/the silver coat with
sable." Its blackness, therefore, makes it vulnerable. The woman
seems to have been attracted to what she considered the animal's
beauty, but what was actually the lemming's curse—its sable
fur. Out of this attraction and out of pity to help the "errantly
lamed" lemming, she is struck. Like the soldiers who provide
the topic of this woman's conversation, this woman, through
her blindness and misapprehension of a situation, has been in-
jured by the very thing she thought beautiful.

Anne Spencer did not believe that men and women are absolutely equal in every sense of the word, but that sexual discrimination in many cases is as outdated in its justification as is the medieval concept of a flat world. She said that when she would hear advocates of women's liberation make such statements as "this is the first time I have felt like a woman, like a human being," she became disgusted because any woman who is a woman at all should have always known that she was a woman and a human being. She strongly believed in women's liberation, but she said that the whole situation had to be put in perspective, that people must understand that men and women never will be "equal," simply because they are of different sexes. She expressed this idea in her poem "Po' Little Lib" (previously titled "Tragedy" and "Garden Incident").

According to the poet, the main point of "Po' Little Lib" is that as long as the female has the job of producing young, male and female never will be equal, which does not imply inferiority of either sex. There are roles that each must play, and one cannot ignore this. The poem in its last stanza expresses the desire of the female spider to be "free"; yet never can she be completely free of exclusively feminine roles:

> Run, escape, wee one you are free . . .
> How delicately she re-knits her vast pain
> Chance did set her free
> What bound her again?

The female spider never can escape the role of having to carry her young, thus "her femaleness binds her, that femininity which unites the universe," said Mrs. Spencer. Actually the poem expresses the strength of the female sex. Anne Spencer said that "there is no telling how many males she has consumed in her life, for after fertilization the female spider destroys the male."

Shortly after observing a spider in her garden, Anne Spencer wrote the first and longer draft of this poem and sent it to Walter White for his appraisal. White was correct in suggesting that the poem be shortened, but "Po' Little Lib" is a good example of what Anne Spencer accomplishes in her poems. The garden incident which sparked "Po' Little Lib" is indeed a familiar observation of a commonplace event developed into a more insightful expression. The poem is not so far removed from the incident which occasioned its composition that one cannot readily see the connection between the germinal idea and the finished poem —that method of poetic composition stated in "1975."

The motivation for the composition of several of her poems is not so obvious in the finished products. "I just don't take these things out of the sky and write them down," she said. "I might have an idea for a poem in my head for a long time before something happens to cause me to write that idea down" in poetic form. Mrs. Spencer talked to me about her individual poems only in terms of the incident or idea which led to the composition of a particular poem or the state of mind which preceded the writing. (She never agreed to explicate one of her poems for me.) She recalled, for example, that she and Edward once took a trip to Harpers Ferry, West Virginia, where she was overjoyed to observe the historical site of John Brown's defiant rebellion against the institution of human slavery in America. At this site she noticed in particular an oak tree covered with mistletoe and shortly afterwards the poem "Creed" took shape, referring directly to the oak and mistletoe she saw at Harpers Ferry and also echoing the sense of human freedom she associated with this historical site.

The short poem "Epitome," said Anne Spencer, reflects her husband's frequent characterization of her. An anecdote she told provides part of the background for the poem. As teenagers her daughters Alroy and Bethel often wanted to attend some function for their age group or do the kind of things girls that age liked to do. They would ask their father for permission; he in turn would say "ask your mother." If Mrs. Spencer withheld her permission, a discussion would ensue as to why the girls could not have permission for the activity in question. At times this discussion would grow to the point where the girls would put their father's tacit approval against their mother's refusal, and Edward would placatingly remark to Alroy and Bethel: "Your mother was never young. She went from childhood to middle (or old) age," Mrs. Spencer recalled. Another anecdote rounds out the background for the poem. The children habitually would ask their father random questions about any subject, as children invariably do. Edward many times would reply: "Ask you mother; she will tell you whether she knows or not." Putting these two characterizations together, Anne Spencer developed "Epitome."

More important than the anecdotal background for this poem, "Epitome" alludes to Anne Spencer's thirst for knowledge, and in that sense is an instance of self-characterization. An avid reader since her years at Virginia Seminary, she found that the more she read and learned, the more she knew there was to learn. The poem's characterization is the epitome of a mind with a little bit of knowledge thinking that she "knew all the answers," but discovering as she grew older and her knowledge increased that "Now the world is old and I am still young/For the young know nothing, nothing."

To a large extent she works with the same themes, imagistic patterns, and traditional forms in her different poems. Nevertheless, the attitudes and approaches she takes to what otherwise would be commonplace and conventional verse distinguish her as a poet of merit. Writing briefly in a headnote to selections of her poetry, the editors of the 1973 edition of *The Norton Anthology of Modern Poetry* comment justly on Anne Spencer as poet: "She is sometimes close to obviousness, with expressions that are nearly trite, but just when she seems to be merely echoing routine feelings, her diction sharpens, and her ideas become fresh and unexpected. The poetry that results has an unassuming sincerity as often graceful as awkward." [15]

Among the several entries in her Notebooks which show her evaluating herself as a poet are two comments which perhaps

15. Richard Ellmann and Robert O'Clair (eds.), *The Norton Anthology of Modern Poetry* (New York: W. W. Norton and Co., 1973), 276.

support the statement above. Commenting on "Grapes: Still-Life," she wrote: "I defend and deploy criticism of excess given lines I wrote years gone, 'Snugly you rest, sweet globes,/Aged essence of the sun'—I'd claim master pattern by Mr. Shakespeare of his 'When to the sessions of sweet silent thought'; but now I say listen to the effective sibilation of Spy Kelly—in any unsafe tight situation!" At one time apparently evaluating her total poetic abilities and accomplishments, she recorded a seemingly hasty and at points unintelligible comment:

Q. Is it unfair to ask you how you rate yourself as a poet?
A. No. As a vibrating human being compelled to [recapture?] the probes of earth pulse and response—
    2. As a re-teller, to [create], cite and deliver, I'm definitive *heavy* 3rd rate
    3. & nearly always a reluctant participant—I'm a [disappointment?] and No. 4

It no doubt would be erroneous to claim that Anne Spencer is a major or even grossly neglected minor American poet in the sense that the terms generally are used. Yet it is true that she is an important American poet. Her significance is not based solely on her infrequent publications of some fine specimens of early twentieth-century poetry, but includes the how, why, and wherefore of her literary career. She is significant in that, given her background and environment and the American cultural system of the time, she never should have been the accomplished poet she became. She had every external force working against her: she was southern; she was a resident of Lynchburg, Virginia, a racially unsettled town with few cultural outlets for its black citizens—not even a library; though her six years of formal education was not as limited in cultural subjects as was that at similar schools, she did not have the college-level training that many writers of the Harlem Renaissance (and of the period) had; for her locale she had an unusual amount of contact with artists and intellectuals during the ten years of her publishing activity, but, unlike many writers during the first third of this century whose talents seem to have been nourished by their membership in a literary coterie or residence in a city with cultural outlets, Anne Spencer was not a member of a sustained literary coterie nor did she live in a culturally active community. In essence, none of the external characteristics of her life, according to unwritten rules of early twentieth-century American society, was supposed to be conducive to writing the kind and quality of poetry she did, when she did.

Anne Spencer is a spokeswoman of beauty, love, and humanity. Her poems do not fit a general category of love poetry, religious poetry, romantic poetry, or the like (though she has close affinities with the nature poets); yet practically all of them contain religious motifs and romantic elements. One tangible characteristic of her poetry is that it is optimistic. As she said in the headnote to her poems in Cullen's *Caroling Dusk*, she was incapable of writing about hatred or negativism. This implies the whole plan of her poetry. She usually starts with doubt, dilemma, uncertainty. Resentful of or rejecting these negatives, she changes the whole mood, tone, and meaning of her poems. The dark images of night, fainting lamps, shadows, and mysterious doubts are usually transformed into songs of hope and optimism, into the beauty of contrasting light and shadow, into the calm and peace of sunsets, into affirmations of love.

In almost every poem there is a clash, a confrontation which usually follows the uncertainty, the doubt, the mysterious. Doubt and agony seem to prevail at the beginning, but as the poem proceeds through the confrontation, that confrontation or clash takes a more elevated course. The end is the triumph of hope and affirmation. This is, however, connected with defiance. It is defiance and determination that bring about the rebirth of a new phase of life, that negate the uncertainty with which the poem began.

Defiance is not only a major motif in Anne Spencer's poetry; it was highly characteristic of her life. This fact may have led some of her critic-friends to call her poetry very personal, private. Yet she is careful enough to absent subjective references, and this gives her poems a universal appeal and significance.

Though there are frequent personal touches, especially references to her husband, children, house and garden, her poems,
nevertheless, tell the story of a group or generation, not only of
an individual. The personal touches become symbolic and universal because they are more humanitarian than personal.

There is suffering in Anne Spencer's poems, but not so much
the sufferings of an individual as of a group or generation. Out
of the sufferings of the generation Anne Spencer visualizes; out
of its wish fulfillment, out of its fears and aspirations, emerges
the voice of the poet expressing its wretched status hopefully
and in an assuring manner. That is not to say that she is sentimental; she is, in fact, more religious than falsely emotional.
However, the prevalent religious aspect of her poetry is not a
conventional religion. It is a personal religion which combines
the pagan and the Christian, the mortal and the divine, the personal and the universal. Her religion is interestingly and differently expressed in such poems as "Creed," "I Have a Friend,"
and "Letter to My Sister."

The many mythological allusions in her poetry no doubt reflect her early training in the classics at Virginia Seminary. The
several conventional (or orthodox) religious allusions reflect in
part her extensive readings in the Bible. And her whole treatment of religious motifs perhaps reflects in part her early days at
the seminary when she had many doubts about Christianity,
when she basically disagreed with the religious doctrine being taught at the seminary, and when at the age of fourteen
and with two years of schooling she wrote her first poem, "The
Skeptic."

Ever since this first awkward attempt to write a poem in 1896,
poetry was an avocation for her which she too infrequently allowed the reading public to share. In April, 1972, Anne Spencer
drafted a prefatory note for those young people, especially black
youth, who might derive any enjoyment or literary encourage-
ment from reading her poems. She said the note was meant to
explain why she wrote and the difficulties black poets in her day
had getting published. Her eyesight was seriously impaired

when she wrote this; some of the words, therefore, are unclear in the draft, but it seems an appropriate ending for a discussion of her poetry.

Dear Children,

While you are no longer Kinder—(do any of us but stupid ones ever grow up?). Thankfully, as we grow we sprout whatever aptitudes each one owns as a life-gift. Back in my day, a few centuries ago, we were far more advanced in Science than the competing labs. are today. It is written down to prove it: once a thing gets printed, it is positive—To Somebody! Useful facts are never—but alas, they are or are not. I am making a half-blind attempt to get to the Science of Mother Goose. Cf.: Ap. [Apollo] 16 is getting ready to begin to go up to fix to a star. In my day, even a creature as ruminant as a cow jumped over the moon & we thought nothing of it! Dishes again got clean again by running away, and the little dogs could laugh (remember how "Tridlum" the terrier [the Spencers' dog] would laugh, tossing his head?). Never believe what Chesterfield wrote in a letter to his son, "laughter has nothing to do with humor," tho he was almost right. The only thing—What I'm trying to beg of you is use your gift—if it's a true one it will have meaning for you and every life yours touches.

Four and 20 Blacks baked in a pie. When a small hole was cut out they did fly.

Love,
Granny

9 ✕ Last Years

After James Weldon Johnson's death in 1938, Anne Spencer slowly began to alter that high level of activity which marked her life during the two previous decades. The subsequent years seem uneventful when compared to those before the 1940s, but completely subdued her life and spirit were not.

By 1945 she had left her job at Dunbar High School and thus further decreased her contacts outside 1313 Pierce. The board of education had become concerned that she did not have a degree in library science, though she had demonstrated her efficiency as a librarian. She had attended institutes in library science at various schools, but without becoming certified. When the board began to hint that she must become certified (after twenty years' experience and at sixty years old), "I quit and came home. They didn't tell me to quit. I knew. People don't have to tell *me* those sort of things." She retired from the school system with the same salary with which she had begun, seventy-five dollars per month. She never received a raise during the twenty years, nor did she receive a pension from the school system once she retired. Strangely enough she never protested this inequity, but said that money was not her object and that she worked at the library in order to be near books and children.

Though Anne Spencer seems to have withdrawn more and more from public life and to have tempered her attacks on Lynchburg's racism after about 1940, she still exercised that "colossal reserve of constructive indignation" and rose on particular occasions to voice dissent over specific issues. From her Notebooks comes the fragmentary draft of a letter which shows her still holding her own and asserting her opinions in a manner with which Lynchburg was familiar. (There are drafts of similar letters among her papers.) Though the fragmented draft does not reveal to whom the letter was written (and I have therefore deleted other names contained in it), there is enough of this draft to help substantiate some of the assertions in Chapter 6 about the fiery spirit of Anne Spencer and her opponents' image of her:

I have your astonishing letter of Nov. 18, 1947. I am writing as a matter of record to express my chagrin at the evidence it portrays of your complete misunderstanding of me as a person, or deliberate desire to place me in the wrong—where no wrong has been done.

My personal chagrin and shock arise from an unsustained charge that I fight everything. It would have been more expected from you if you had accused me of being a person who speaks her mind forthrightly and refuses to resort to subterfuge.

. . . Whatever [way?] that's necessary I take. So I will not mention the names of the two other teachers who heard you say—I shall not attempt to quote your exact words, but this is your meaning as said to the three of us. [The material in question here is not included in the draft.] I was literal enough to believe that you meant what you said.

For the moment I am not discussing Mr.——. Now, for Mr.——, I here record my belief in the integrity of any work he would undertake to do as shown by the expert passion for detail and the good finished job of whatever he has undertaken through the years. No one could doubt my sincerity in this instance unless he deliberately bypassed the obvious. . . .

So far as the complete meaning of the letter went, it was mine, although I did not write it alone. So complete was I in sympathy with what it said that that sentiment is still final.

As for those who signed it, they are literate and did not sign without reading. They are sane and I do not expect any one of them to rescind it. No one was approached who did not have some special stake in the progress of our schools.

Since you yourself, by your own words, deplored to see any more jerry-built housing go up around these environs, and since all of us by our very presence here are devoted to the objective of realizing in the education of our children equal physical and spiritual facilities, the letter written in part by me and subscribed to by those we felt were in a position to have the most interest in this question, [should make each of us] willing to support the other in a just contention. . . . The letter written in part by me was heartily subscribed to by the signers with thanks for the opportunity.

Having curtailed the more public side of their life, Anne and Edward—now fondly called Mother and Pop by neighbors, friends, and family—lived alone in the privacy and serenity of 1313 Pierce Street from the mid-1940s to 1964. Literary friends and other associates the Spencers had met in the 1920s continued to visit 1313 Pierce and kept in contact until failing health and age prevented their travels, decreased the number of their letters, and one by one they died. Georgia Douglas Johnson and Langston Hughes were among the last of that 1920s circle to break the fraternal bond with 1313 Pierce Street when they died in 1966 and 1967, respectively. By the 1970s, only Anne Spencer and Grace N. Johnson (Mrs. James Weldon Johnson) remained.

Witnessing a delightful and vigorous style of life diminish—trips to such cities as New York, Washington, and Atlanta; a house filled with guests, famed and familiar; parties in and out of season; quiet summer visits from friends—Anne and Edward became more and more absorbed with watching the number of their grandchildren and great-grandchildren increase and with enjoying the pleasure of cultivating their garden, which was indeed in its greatest splendor. It was during this twenty-year period that Edward gained quite a bit of attention in the local papers for the varied and attractive birdhouses he built.

In 1947 Mrs. Spencer's mother, Sarah Scales Dickerson, died. Both Mrs. Spencer's parents remarried after about 1900. In 1902 Sarah married James Dickerson, a "coke boss" in a mine near Bramwell, West Virginia. Mr. Dickerson died a few years after the marriage, and about 1920 Mrs. Dickerson came to live at 1313 Pierce Street, where she remained until her death.

Mrs. Spencer's sporadic yet intense involvement with local human rights groups and the attention and some hostility she drew from her anti-integration stand concerning public schools in the late 1950s seem to stand out most in her life for this decade. Her efforts and her outspoken derision of racial attitudes had alienated her from both whites and blacks in Lynchburg, but that never frightened or silenced her. She recalled times in Lynchburg when racial tension was high because school integration appeared imminent. "If the Klan tried to burn a cross on my yard, they'd have to shoot me dead," she said with determination. When school integration did come to Lynchburg, Anne Spencer fought it. She never had approved of Jim Crow schools; yet she was not in favor of tokenism. And she fought "the integration of school, but not by race. What they were offering was not perfection. While they were putting one Negro child in an 'integrated' school, they were continuing to dig a hole out of a hole and build a Jim Crow school."

After the schools were integrated in Lynchburg, several "integrated functions" were held in the town, the most notable of which included many prominent black and white citizens—"the integrationists," in Mrs. Spencer's words. She was not invited. A reporter from the local paper called at her home to get her reaction to having been excluded from the esteemed affair. "They had a right not to invite me because I fought them tooth and nail," she told the reporter. She said she told the young woman several other things, but reflected that "less than half of what you tell a reporter ever gets printed."

Anne Spencer said that a good friend of hers, Arthur P. Davis, characterized her as a private person (though in a somewhat different context than the one used here).[1] "I'm not a private person, I'm *me*," she said. If indeed her individualism over the years had caused her friends to see her as a private person, if her life and opinions had caused the people of Lynchburg to regard her as a rebel, an agitator, or an egoist, they no doubt had failed to understand the workings of the mind and actions of a person seemingly fully aware of the intricacies of life and the role she had to play in a human environment with which she clashed. One might add, then, that Anne Spencer was by nature a rebel in the positive sense, a person who defied any limitations on her freedom as a human being, and who was always a champion for the underdog. That defiance which seemed to have been a natu-

1. Arthur P. Davis and Saunders Redding (eds.), *Cavalcade: Negro American Writing from 1760 to the Present* (Boston: Houghton Mifflin Co., 1971), 269.

ral part of her is interestingly expressed by the speaker of her poem "Creed":

> I may challenge God when we meet That Day,
> And He dare not be silent or send me away.

There is little doubt that Anne Spencer was an individualist—which, unfortunately, some people viewed negatively. And it was just that particular brand of individualism which motivated her humanitarianism and caused many Lynchburg citizens and organizations to ostracize her more and more after her stand against integration. By the early 1960s she had withdrawn even more into her private world.

Out of the decade of the 1960s it was 1962 which she loved to recall, both for its pains and joys. That year Edward was 86 and Anne was 80. An abdominal tumor which grew rapidly necessitated her hospitalization and eventual surgery. Because the tumor's growth was unusually large, because her black hair had only a few gray streaks, and because she exhibited a generally youthful appearance, she was mistaken for a maternity patient. (I would suspect, however, that this incident occurred before 1962.) After the operation her hair began to turn gray and facial lines of age began to appear to an extent that she no longer appeared to be twenty or thirty years younger than she actually was.

1964 probably was the most painful year of her eighty-two-year life, after which she wished for the peace and joy death would bring. It was late one cold night during the 1963/64 winter when Anne awoke to find Edward out of bed and struggling on the floor with the blanket which had fallen from her bed and warning her to keep it in place because the night was unseasonably cold and damp. Edward's late-night wandering through the house and his grappling on the floor with the blanket caused Anne some concern when during the following days she noticed other aspects of his actions and manner which were not consistent with his usual demeanor. Before long she began to suspect that Edward's physical and mental selves were losing strength. To increase her fears, the blanket scene was repeated on later occasions—once when the blanket was not on the floor. This last time it was not a cold winter night, and Anne awoke to find that Ed, as he had done previously, was out of bed and apparently returning from the bathroom. He dropped to the floor beside her bed and began trying, awkwardly, to pull up a blanket that was not there and telling her that she must keep it on the bed. She knew then, to be sure, that he was rapidly approaching death; for some time now his mind had begun to wander and his physical agility had markedly deteriorated.

It was not long after this that on the morning of May 17, 1964, Edward Alexander Spencer died. Anne Spencer ever since felt a tremendously tragic loss, probably more than most people feel at the death of a spouse. On the editorial page of the Lynchburg *News* for May 19, 1964, a memorial expressed what no doubt many felt at the death of one of Lynchburg's most respected citizens:

The death of Edward A. Spencer at the age of 88 years removes one of Lynchburg's most respected, exemplary citizens, to all who knew him well enough to be aware of his quality.

One of the accomplishments characterizing him was his acquisition and approval of rental property so that the area was called Spencer Place in official recognition, and was sometimes referred to as an initiatory, private, housing development in the city.

For older citizens the Spencer family needs no introduction. And it is pertinent to note here, though she modestly might not wish it, that his widow has for very many years had national publishing and critical recognition as a poet, and the Spencer family were often host to leading Negro writers, editors and musicians, though her recognition was not confined to them or their publications.

In expressing sympathy for Mr. Spencer's family we recall the strong friendship of Mrs. Martha Adams, for so many years with this newspaper, for the Spencers and respect for their contribution to the better life of the community.

It is good to know Edward A. Spencer was appreciated and that widespread sympathy will go to his survivors, family and friends. Gentle, generous, kindly, honorable and with a sensitive intelligence, such men live on in memory.

The loss was almost more than Anne Spencer could bear, and after the funeral she left her home for the first extended absence since moving there and went to live with her daughter Bethel. Six months later she returned to 1313 Pierce Street—"for Pop's spirit and influence were there"—and vowed never to leave again if any way she could prevent doing so. "He was a man, a husband, a father and a *friend*," she said. "Pop just let me do what I wanted. If I liked it, he did too. Pop was so good to me that everything I did he entered into it." She wrote a special poem about their relationship (one of those unpublished and unseen ones) and his presence is evident in many of her earlier poems. The year following his death, the theme of death seemed to have been foremost in her mind, and she reflected this in her notes and "scribblings."

From 1965 to 1972 Anne Spencer lived alone in her Pierce Street home and resisted all pleas from her children to leave Lynchburg or at least allow someone to stay with her as nurse and housekeeper. For over sixty years she had lived at 1313 Pierce and for most of that time she had fought Lynchburg. She would not leave Pierce Street or Lynchburg voluntarily. She loved her home too much to leave it and she hated Lynchburg too much to leave it alone. She was as much a part of her house as were its furnishings and books. She had fought the town, the newspaper, the people (black and white), and the imbedded racism in Lynchburg most of her adult life. Though she spoke of it with disgust, she and the town were like old enemies, almost too fond of each other to part company. Of the comments in her Notebooks about Lynchburg, a brief notation, perhaps written in the 1950s, tends to characterize her lifelong "war" with the town: "Once before I asked Lybg a question: What are we willing to die for? 20 years and later it is what are we willing to *Live* for?"

Though her focus most often was Lynchburg, her war against the inhumanity of man to man frequently extended beyond the borders of Lynchburg and Virginia: "Once, 2 or 3 years back, I got so mad at Henry Garrett, Ph.D., I threw away one dollar and 67 cents on him. I put in a tracer call to [Columbia University?] for a Dr. Garrett—possibly consulting a category. No, I said, he is not an MD but a head shrinker—his own. I got him! That man has a spiteful attitude [unchanging] toward creation" (Notebooks).[2] The passage is indicative of Mrs. Spencer's determination never to allow what she considered injustice, bigotry, or inhumanity to go unchallenged. If, for example, she became outraged by a statement she read or by one which she heard on radio or television, she seldom would hesitate to call the author of the statement "to give him a piece of my mind." Many times she never was able to speak to the person, for her targets in these instances included heads of local and national agencies as well as governmental officials; whoever happened to be president of the United States at the time was not excluded.

Though her children persisted that she leave Lynchburg, Mrs. Spencer remained in control of her life, and left her home and town only briefly on occasions when it was absolutely necessary to do so. Even during the last year of her life she vehemently opposed any suggestion of a nurse taking care of her as long as she was not confined to bed. Sometime in the late 1960s, one of her daughters tried to force a nurse on her. Plans were made and the nurse was brought into the home. A few people thought—and the children hoped—that at last Mrs. Spencer's determined will had been at least bent. The daughter left Lynchburg to return to her own home; yet before her flight had landed , Mrs. Spencer "had given the nurse her walking papers." In the

---

2. Henry E. Garrett, Ph.D., was for sixteen years head of the psychology department at Columbia University. A staunch advocate and author of numerous articles promoting the theory of the inherent inferiority of black Americans, Garrett often is considered the chief spokesman of the school of "scientific racists" who were quite vocal in the 1950s and 1960s, a group which included Wesley C. George of the University of North Carolina, Audrey M. Shuey of Randolph-Macon College (Lynchburg, Virginia), Frank McGurk of Villanova University, and Carleton Putman, one-time businessman, sometime historian and scientist. Of this group of "scientific racists," Audrey M. Shuey, based in Lynchburg, was easily accessible to Anne Spencer's attacks on those who promoted the theory of black inferiority, especially after the publication in 1958 of her book *The Testing of Negro Intelligence*.

draft of a letter to a friend (perhaps Mrs. James Weldon Johnson) about the nurse, Mrs. Spencer wrote: "I was *weller* than she!"

I first met Mrs. Spencer in March, 1971, after she consented to give me an interview. She was not particularly eager to talk about her writings and preferred to "talk life" (not necessarily hers), her conversation encompassing many topics, people, and events. During that first meeting she informed me that she had written much more than had been published, and she talked briefly about a very few of the "thousand or so" poems she said she had written for her own enjoyment. At that time she kindly and politely refused any further interviews; six months later she tacitly agreed to talk more extensively about her life and writings. During the next three years she became more and more interested in the project. She gradually began to try to assemble and organize her writings and to recall incidents which she felt were pertinent to a biographical-critical study.

Though the process was slow, within eighteen months after our first meeting I had collected a general biographical sketch and had uncovered some previously unpublished poems. It was several months after she agreed to the study that I learned many of her poems were not available, in that some time before a group of young boys had vandalized the garden house in her backyard where she kept many of literary papers. But now thoroughly interested in the project, she tried to reconstruct the poems which had been destroyed by the vandalism.

She also decided that if a study were to be done of her life, she would like to have as much control over it as possible. She preferred to write down her recollections because she wanted things said a certain way. She discouraged note-taking (though she never said not to take notes) and she disliked tape recorders (she disliked her voice on them and was afraid that she might say something on tape which she could not retract). After she decided that she would do a large amount of the work herself, I collected little during my many visits with her and they became just that: pleasant visits to a dear friend. Though she would readily talk about several unpublished poems she had written, often quoting lines or sections from them, she would not allow me to take them away or to copy them. She wanted to wait until she had them "just right." This process worked well for a while; then her eyesight began to deteriorate rapidly. She then asked a young lady who lived nearby to type some of the poems and notes on which she was working. The young lady did an admirable job; but, unable to read much of Mrs. Spencer's writing (I suspect), she could do little with organizing, deciphering, and transcribing what Mrs. Spencer had written. By 1973 Anne Spencer could not see the paper well enough to write in a straight line and would often write off the page or write over words and lines previously written. My somewhat modest urgings to let me help with the paper work went unheeded; instead, she bought larger pencils and wider tablets, but the problem persisted.

When Mrs. Spencer accepted the fact that her poor eyesight was seriously restraining her physical efforts and the strong possibility that total blindness was imminent, for the first time, in the spring of 1973, she allowed me to "plow through some old boxes of trash"—a part of her "filing system"—and there I found a few more poem manuscripts and several interesting letters. It is likely that she knew exactly what was in those boxes— or what was not in them—and still held in reserve other accumulations of papers which no doubt contained significant writings.

Feeling particularly well in late May, 1973, she took a trip to the countryside with friends for a picnic. A few days after this, a couple of her friends and neighbors, who looked in on her periodically, noticed that she was not her usual self and that she had taken to her bed. When her condition did not improve but worsened, the neighbors notified her family; Bethel came to Lynchburg and hospitalized her mother. The family doctor recommended major surgery to remove an obstruction in her intestines. The attending physicians gave her less than a fifty-fifty chance to survive the necessary surgery. For two or three weeks after the surgery doctors showed little optimism for her recovery.

But by September and October she had amazed everyone who had seen her in June after the operation by what appeared to be a remarkable recovery.

As a result of her illness and recuperation, family and friends came to 1313 Pierce Street and someone was hired to stay with her. During the months of her recuperation it is likely that many of her papers innocently were discarded. Certainly no one deliberately threw away any of her writings; but anyone unfamiliar with her methods of composition and filing would not know what was and what was not important. Her system was clear only to her. Any time a thought crossed her mind she would write it down. On paper bags, in the margins and fly leaves of books, on envelopes, in tablets, on the telephone bill, on the back of a check, a new line to a poem, a revision of a line, an entire poem, data about her life, or just "thoughts" would appear. This habit of "jotting down things here, there and everywhere" perhaps began as early as the 1890s. She would know exactly where some bit of information was recorded; to the unfamiliar eye a scrap of paper with a few scribblings was waste to be discarded (especially if the paper was old and worn). The central problem, therefore, is that not only are valuable papers lost but there are fragments of several things which are probably useless now if indeed the other parts are missing. What survived of these "scribblings" form the bulk of what I term her Notebooks; they reveal much about the life and mind of Anne Spencer.

Mrs. Spencer, I suspect, immersed herself more deeply into reading and writing during the decade following Edward's death in 1964 than at any similar period in her life. If what is available of her notes is any indication of her thought process during this period, her "mind brooded on history," especially on the "peculiar institution" of American slavery. Though some of the "scribblings on history and slavery" date back as far as the 1920s, this interest intensified during the last decade of her life. And for the first time in her life she was much more interested in writing prose than poetry.

Perhaps it was in the mid-1960s (judging from the unsteadiness of the hand) that she recorded the following: "When I was young with a younger family, I was a scrap paper scribbler in pencil, so now there is nothing save a whetted gnawing hope of doing what *the* H. L. Mencken advised me once: Prose pieces my mind has chewed on for a decade or so." When I first met her in 1971 she said that she had almost completed a long historical prose piece. Motivated by several things—the works of Harriet Beecher Stowe (who, Mrs. Spencer maintained, gathered some of her material for *Uncle Tom's Cabin* from Virginia), the works of Virginia novelists (especially James Branch Cabell), the writings of southern historians, recent articles in the local paper, and Allen Tate's classic essay of self-analysis, "Narcissus as Narcissus" (probably as a frame), among other things—Mrs. Spencer's article, I gather, covered many aspects of the position of blacks in the history of Virginia, of the South, and of the nation. In 1972 she said the article was complete except for the opening sentence, which she soon composed. She would cite several passages from the article in our conversations, but I never saw the piece, finally titled "Virginia as Narcissus: In the Best Tradition of Slavery." Drafts of the article have turned up in some recently found material, however.

It is a plausible conclusion that many of the notes on history and slavery in her Notebooks were "thoughts" for or found their way into this article. Some of these notes and her comments about the article and the subject of history reveal a derisive attitude toward what she considered the typical historian's view of American history and slavery: a vainglorious and deliberate misrepresentation of the truth, an attempt to escape history. She recorded:

When history books tell no lies at all, they will be read even less than they are read today. The reader's mind—if so—must amalgamate, or reverse the terms of the divisor and proceed as in multiplication—if I recall what that most earnest teacher said to my nitwithead way back in the nineteenth century. He even tried to explain *why*. The only part of it I did get was ME. He said every result that could be proved was a fact. And there I was. Today in the twentieth century here I am. Here, Mr. Du Bois.

But historians are only one component in a seemingly ordered intellectual and psychological conspiracy to escape history. The narcissistic reader finds solace in history as illusion, history not so much as myth but as lie: "Whatever our sphere or station—let us therefore brace ourselves to our duty—fellow citizens, we cannot escape history in honor or dishonor" (Notebooks). But even worse than the historian as mythmaker or the reader in pursuit of illusion are those who deliberately distort truth: "Humanity is divided thru the middle into true and false liars. Only those people are true liars who will to tell a lie where one is not called for." Anne Spencer records that in the main our historians have obscured history with a conglomeration of meaningless "facts": "History books of men and events must of course be dated by the year of a certain act or action, by the day on which it happened. Even at times by the face on the clock. But while history is not necessarily the complete truth, truth is an important part of history and needs no date." To be sure Anne Spencer is not singular among writers in seeing the records of history as lie, distortion, evasion; for as Ralph Ellison states in *Invisible Man*, "History records the patterns of men's lives, they say: Who slept with whom and with what results; who fought and who won and who lived to lie about it afterwards. . . . those lies his keepers keep their power by."[3] Still close to Ellison's (and other writers') conception of the boomerang effect of American history, Mrs. Spencer noted: "My country is having a hard and agonizing time: whenever any hierocracy seeks stabilizing greatness for itself, it writes an open-eyed invitation to the enemies of its own creation. They attend the party as the 13th fairy—which, if you know your Grimm, always brought hate and the attempt to curse and blight."

Some of the notations on this subject are more specific and deal with the love-hate relationship Anne Spencer saw between blacks and whites in this country:

---

3. Ralph Ellison, *Invisible Man* (New York: Random House, 1952), 332.

When Lee & Grant shook hands in the parlor of the McLean House April 9, 1865, they became brothers again, "making up." But they and their siblings were much less brother & sister than four millions of enslaved people come, tentatively, into their unbondage. The blacks, the shepherd checks, and whites—we were all there and we all had this unique kinship. The separation came gradually. The divorce has never been conceded on either side. We are saturated with memories of each other, making us both reluctant to let go. This I think is love—and often it is, psychologically, loved raised to the point of hatred.

In other notes she touched upon various racial myths and upon the ultimate national taboo: "For not every white in the South struck Negroes or struck oil—many, as now, were themselves struck by poverty & ignorance more dire than that of the slaves. Then there was God's mistake to contend with: The holder saw his female slave as a female to take and took her while his own females saw the often strong Samboys with a deep sense of exquisite contempt and hunger—shuddering." Succinctly characterizing the narcissistic male-dominated South, she wrote: "Southern man is a survival of the southern woman that slavery created in its own image: To be natural is to be false."

From the mid-1950s the subject of history seems to have been almost an obsession with her, and the topic of American slavery found its way directly and indirectly into many things she wrote —letters to various people and organizations, prose pieces (at least three unpublished articles she wrote in the late 1940s for a proposed newspaper column survive), and her "scribblings." Many of the poems on which she worked were within a general historical context. She mentioned having planned a series of poems on generals (the term *general* to be more specifically defined by the poems' content), and she drafted a short prose piece titled "What Makes a General?" The generals in this planned series included Hannibal, Napoleon, and Douglas MacArthur, as well as Abraham Lincoln, John Brown, and LeRoi Jones (Imamu Amiri Baraka). Drafts and notes for these poems are in varying degrees of completion (though none is complete), ranging from prose notations about certain poems to tentative titles, lines, couplets, quatrains, and stanzas. "Bastion at Newark" (which also is the title of what appears to be a short story on the same subject) concerns LeRoi Jones. "LeRoi Meets Lincoln" was planned as a dramatic monologue in which LeRoi Jones stands before the Lincoln Memorial and meditates on history.

The most complete manuscript in this group of poems is the several hundred lines of verse and notes for the planned five-canto "A Dream of John Brown: On His Return Trip Home." In late 1972 Mrs. Spencer feared that her impaired eyesight was a forewarning of complete blindness, so she abandoned all her writing projects to work exclusively on "John Brown," an idea which she first conceived as early as the 1920s. She devoted so much attention to this effort—her "masterpiece"—that she further weakened her health and lost her vision almost entirely before giving up the project two years later. Parts of what she completed were ordered and typed. Numerous other lines and notes are scattered in book margins, on scraps of paper, and so on, with little indication of exactly where these scattered parts would fit into the whole. (I'm sure other parts were discarded with the trash.)

Suggested by William Morris' "A Dream of John Ball," Anne Spencer's "A Dream of John Brown" was planned as a dream in which the poet witnesses Brown's hanging (1859), his transformation from "hu-man" life to spiritual essence. God has sent John Brown on a mission to earth. Having determined that Brown's mission has been completed, He calls him home to heaven. The poet's dream-vision monitors the return trip.

The poet uses at least three different but interrelated concepts of time in the poem's thematic and structural development. Basically, each of the structural-thematic concepts of time emanates from one of the poem's three main speakers: the poet (dream time), John Brown (human time), and God (cosmic time). Dream time provides the outer frame for the poem, and consists of the spatial juxtaposition of events or actions as they occur in the mind when it is in a dream state, when chronology as the conscious mind knows it is no longer the interval by which one measures or orders events. The second concept, human time, functions primarily as a gauge for patterning and ordering earthly events. With John Brown as its pivot, human time encompasses man's history on earth, which the poet relates thematically rather than chronologically. The third concept of time, cosmic time, thematically includes dream time and human time. God is the touchstone by which cosmic time is effected in the poem. Cosmic time enables the poet to span the historical chronology of past, present, and future, and to demonstrate thematically the relationship between different events in human history, between man and his universe, and between man's universe and the cosmic scheme.

Though it includes world history, the poem is deeply rooted in American history and American slavery, with John Brown's hanging used as a thematic core. Each of the three main speakers organizes, synthesizes, and interprets history from his particular perspective of time. In addition to providing the primary thematic focus, John Brown's hanging, by analogy, is the chief technical device of the poem. As he swings back and forth on the gallows, Brown symbolically becomes a pendulum of history. Underlying the human pendulum as a death symbol is the idea that death (the cessation of vital functions) does not occur instantaneously, but that the dying process is a gradual transition from human life to nonhuman life. When all vital functions have ceased, the transition from human life to spiritual essence is complete. In addition, the poem's structure utilizes a generally held concept that during the dying process one can, within a fraction of human chronology, span an almost infinite period of time, past and future. Asserting that during the dying process one is no longer completely within the confines of earth time, the poet uses the two ideas above, along with the suggestion that when dreaming the mind is not confined by earthly chronology, to comment on all human history within a cosmic context. The historical themes, the rhythmic structures, and the chief symbol merge; form and meaning coalesce.

As John Brown swings, he moves from human time to cosmic

time. When the John Brown-pendulum swings left to the vertical point, he is within human time and the poet is able to relate past and present historical events as well as Brown's biographical data that occur within this earthly chronology. The farther left the pendulum swings, the farther back into history (pre-1859) the poet goes in her thematic synthesis and interpretation. As the pendulum begins to swing right toward the vertical point, the poet continues relating Brown's biography and events of history that were omitted during the leftward swing, still avoiding a strict chronology and further ordering history thematically.

At the vertical position life stops. The "hu-man" enters a state of death as the pendulum swings from vertical to right. It is during this rightward movement that the poet relates, in a physical sense, Brown's journey through the universe toward the throne of God. In these sections Mrs. Spencer makes frequent use of mythology, astrology, and astronomy. When John Brown reaches the throne of God (the pendulum at its farthest point right), the poet now views history, the earth, and the universe as they fit within the divine cosmic scheme. With this techinque she is able to comment on the future from a cosmic perspective (in the dialogue between John Brown and God). This left-to-right movement provides both the technical and thematic structures of the poem and continues in tick-tock rhythmic motion until the dream is over, John Brown has been transformed completely from human form to spiritual essence, and man's past, present, and future history has been concluded. When the poem ends, "Vega comes up to unite the world"; harmony pervades the entire universe.

Anne Spencer's use of time is one of several interesting aspects of this poem. The interpretative analyses and poetic use of history are intriguing. Had she been physically able to execute her plans for this poem, Anne Spencer probably would have distinguished herself as one of the very few American poets to write competent poetry past the age of ninety.

Among her Notebooks there are ideas for and remnants of

other poems on which she worked before becoming absorbed with "John Brown." The fragments reveal the varying topics which occupied her mind during the last decade of her life—that matter from which she could "make a poem." Included are: a nearly finished poem on Ruth Brown (rock and roll singer popular during the 1950s); notes for and a poem about astronauts and man's relationship to the universe; "O Pinions," a poem about the poet's (Anne Spencer's) place in the universe; nature poems; poems about words and language; and a very interesting piece (with drafts in prose and poetry) titled "Stanchion Roots," whose narrative substance concerns incestuous miscegenation and the complete lack of control a young male slave has over his life. (The poem is based on autobiographical anecdotes an old man told Mrs. Spencer when she was a young woman.)

It is unfortunate that so many of Anne Spencer's "scribblings" have been lost. If more of these items were available, one could reconstruct a fascinating record of the mind, life, times, and making of the poet. I suspect that each day she recorded several of her thoughts during, say, at least the last fifty years of her life. Probably most of her poems grew out of the random notes she scribbled here, there, and everywhere. Indeed, from the items available, one can determine her usual method of poetic composition by tracing, in more than one instance, the uncontrived step-by-step process she used to develop her "scribbled thoughts" into poetry—from recorded germinal idea to expanded thought, and then from crude verse to polished poem.

At the end of 1973 her writing activities came to an abrupt halt. In January, 1974, her doctor declared a soreness in her mouth and throat to be a potentially malignant condition. She went to New York the first week in March and underwent surgery, which at first seemed to have arrested the cancer but which left her practically bald (much of her hair had fallen out after the June, 1973, operation) and her speech muddled, since part of her tongue had to be removed and replaced with artificial fiber. Within two weeks after this operation, the doctors removed cataracts from her eyes, and her improved eyesight compensated somewhat for the speech impediment.

By late May she had convinced her doctors and her children that she "was well enough now to be allowed to come home to be with Pop." Her daughter Bethel accompanied her to Lynchburg. A few weeks in her Lynchburg home and Mrs. Spencer gradually persuaded Bethel to allow her to live alone. Except for a neighbor, Mrs. Elliot, who assisted her periodically with the chores of maintaining a household, Anne Spencer again enjoyed the freedom and privacy of 1313 Pierce.

From June to December of 1974 she did not find it difficult living alone and, on the whole, caring for herself. However, her blurred eyesight caused mishaps as she moved through her house. At least twice during this period she stumbled and fell, bruising her head in one instance and bruising her hip in another. And contrary to what she had led her doctors and family to believe, the soreness in her mouth and throat never ceased giving her trouble. She exacted from me a promise not to reveal to her family the extent of pain she suffered during these months, nor her minor accidents in the house. She dreaded having her privacy invaded or having to be hospitalized again, and maintained that nothing could be done to correct her medical problem. In addition, she did not want her infirmities to create a burden for her children. "My Dear, I feel your words beating on my head. In the process, too, your heart understands. I'm here now because I'm very aged, very sick, and can't help carrying it over to my dear kin—all the worse because wordless," she wrote in her Notebooks, perhaps in the late fall of 1974.

In June she wrote "1975," suspecting that it would be her last finished poem. "One way or another, I will die in 1975, even if I just have to stop eating," she said, commenting on the significance of the poem's title. "A hundred years is too long to live, and I'm tired!" she continued, laughing. For the past two years her optometrist had refused to prescribe magnifying aids for her

reading, and had warned her that such strain on her sight probably would cause complete blindness. But in June, "with one
good eye and two pairs of glasses," plus various magnifying
aids ("some by prescription and some by crook"), she continued
as much as possible her lifelong practices of reading and writing. In July she resumed work on "John Brown," hoping to fin-
ish it within a year. And, except for a poem she began in the fall
about her husband Edward (titled "Reliques" and planned as a
companion piece to "Po' Little Lib"), after July she abandoned
all her other writing activities and worked exclusively on "John
Brown" for the next six months.

The pain in her mouth and throat steadily increased, so that
by December she found it difficult to eat without experiencing
intense pain. Her appetite decreased. She lost weight. By January, 1975, she was suffering at times excruciating pain in her
mouth and throat, and, her body markedly weakened, she began to remain in bed about twenty hours a day. Bethel came to
Lynchburg and immediately registered her mother in a hospital,
where Mrs. Spencer was nursed back to relatively stable health.
When the hospital released her, Mrs. Spencer was too weak to
climb the stairs to her bedroom as she had done for almost three
quarters of a century. She had pointed out that her ability to
climb two flights of stairs several times each day was an indication that she was basically healthy and self-sufficient, but now
she was confined to a bed set up in her study downstairs. When
Mrs. Spencer could no longer deny that she needed professional
nursing that she could not obtain at home, she, sadly, agreed to
enter a nursing facility in Lynchburg, where she soon adjusted
to her surroundings and did not protest having to leave 1313
Pierce.

While she was in the nursing home her physical condition
fluctuated; about two months after having entered the home,
she again had to be hospitalized. All her life she had dreaded
hospitals, and she was anxious to be discharged from this one at
the earliest possible moment. But this time she looked forward
to returning to the nursing home rather than to her own house

—an indication that she had resigned herself to the imperatives of her physical condition.

On May 8, 1975, Virginia Seminary and College honored the seventy-fourth anniversary of her graduation (she was its oldest living graduate) by conferring upon her an honorary doctor of letters degree ("an ornery degree," Mrs. Spencer reported with a chuckle), but Anne Spencer was too weak to attend the ceremony. The honorary degree certainly revived her spirits, and her physical condition seemed to improve as she showed signs of rejuvenating her former self. Her humor, repartee, and general attitude had made her a favorite of many of the nursing home personnel; her honorary degree boosted her standing to that approaching celebrity. For the next two months her strength fluctuated, but then slowly ebbed. Her acute and lucid mind (except when she was heavily sedated) remained ever intact. At 4:30 P.M. on Saturday, July 27, Anne Spencer died quietly with, as Bethel said, a look of "pleasure, satisfaction, and triumph."

Appendix: The Poems

Although Anne Spencer referred to having written over a thousand poems, only about fifty items are now available as complete poems or significant fragments, forty-two of which are included in this appendix.

During the last years of her life, Mrs. Spencer revised some of her poems from their originally published versions, and the poems are printed here with her final revisions. I have arranged the poems that follow in the thematic order in which I discussed them in Chapters 7 and 8.

1975[1]

Turn an earth clod
Peel a shaley rock
In fondness molest a curly worm
Whose *familiar* is everywhere
Kneel
And the curly worm   sentient *now*
Will *light* the word that tells the poet what a poem is

1. Composed in June, 1974.

Substitution[2]

Is Life itself but many ways of thought,
How real the tropic storm or lambent breeze
Within the slightest convolution wrought
Our mantled world and men-freighted seas?
God thinks . . . and being comes to ardent things:
The splendor of the day-spent sun, love's birth,—
Or dreams a little, while creation swings
The circle of His mind and Time's full girth . . .
As here within this noisy peopled room
My thought leans forward . . . quick! you're lifted clear
Of brick and frame to moonlit garden bloom,—
Absurdly easy, now, our walking, dear,
Talking, my leaning close to touch your face . . .
His All-Mind bids us keep this sacred place!

At the Carnival[3]

Gay little Girl-of-the-Diving-Tank,
I desire a name for you,
Nice, as a right glove fits;
For you—who amid the malodorous
Mechanics of this unlovely thing,
Are darling of spirit and form.
I know you—a glance, and what you are
Sits-by-the-fire in my heart.
My Limousine-Lady knows you, or
Why does the slant-envy of her eye mark
Your straight air and radiant inclusive smile?
Guilt pins a fig-leaf; Innocence is its own adorning.
The bull-necked man knows you—this first time
His itching flesh sees form divine and vibrant health,
And thinks not of his avocation.

2. Revised in 1973 from the version as first published in Countee Cullen (ed.), *Caroling Dusk: An Anthology of Verse by Negro Poets* (New York: Harper, 1927), 48.

3. First published in James Weldon Johnson (ed.), *The Book of American Negro Poetry* (New York: Harcourt, Brace and Co., 1922), 169–70.

I came incuriously—
Set on no diversion save that my mind
Might safely nurse its brood of misdeeds
In the presence of a blind crowd.
The color of life was gray.
Everywhere the setting seemed right
For my mood!
Here the sausage and garlic booth
Sent unholy incense skyward;
There a quivering female-thing
Gestured assignations, and lied
To call it dancing;
There, too, were games of chance
With chances for none;
But oh! the Girl-of-the-Tank, at last!
Gleaming Girl, how intimately pure and free
The gaze you send the crowd,
As though you know the dearth of beauty
In its sordid life.
We need you—my Limousine-Lady,
The bull-necked man, and I.
Seeing you here brave and water-clean,
Leaven for the heavy ones of earth,
I am swift to feel that what makes
The plodder glad is good; and
Whatever is good is God.
The wonder is that you are here;
I have seen the queer in queer places,
But never before a heaven-fed
Naiad of the Carnival-Tank!
Little Diver, Destiny for you,
Like as for me, is shod in silence;
Years may seep into your soul
The bacilli of the usual and the expedient;
I implore Neptune to claim his child to-day!

Rime for the Christmas Baby
(At 48 Webster Place, Orange)[4]

Dear Bess,

> He'll have rings and linen things,
> And others made of silk;
> There'll be toys like other boys'
> And cream upon his milk;
> True, some sort of merit in a mart
> Where goods are sold for money,
> But packed with comfort is the heart
> That shares with you what's funny;
> So please kiss him when he's very bad
> And laugh with him in gladness,—
> Life is too long a way to go,
> And age will bring him sadness . . .
> Pray you for unceasing springs,
> Swelling deep in pard'n
> That into twin lives may grow
> Time's unfading garden.

We Remember
The Rev. Philip F. Morris
A Lott Carey Founder
–1923–

> You have gone out, Phil, darling,
> Through the door in the dawning East,
> And the world is poor by lesser men,
> The censer mourns its priest
>
> Whose own soul lit the taper,
> Himself answered his own prayers
> That many another mortal
> Might climb the radiant stairs;

---

4. First published in *Opportunity: A Journal of Negro Life*, V (December, 1927), 368.

That the glory of things eternal,
That the beauty we freely may dream
Might lift the burdens too heavy,
    Might fix a too transient beam

For the many stumbling in darkness;
For the dull unquickened who live,
For the unloved or those who hated,—
    He gave them that they might give.

Not sad of mien, not too humble,
Nor the "Word" more soft than real;
Love was your Gospel's body,
    But all its bones were steel;

If your mantle fell, O Philip,
If your place must be filled so,—
The Hours bide, the marchers wait,
    Till another child can grow!

Lady, Lady[5]

Lady, Lady, I saw your face,
Dark as night withholding a star . . .
The chisel fell, or it might have been
You had borne so long the yoke of men.
Lady, Lady, I saw your hands,
Twisted, awry, like crumpled roots,
Bleached poor white in a sudsy tub,
Wrinkled and drawn from your rub-a-dub.
Lady, Lady, I saw your heart,
And altared there in its darksome place
Were the tongues of flames the ancients knew,
Where the good God sits to spangle through.

5. First published in the *Survey's Graphic Number*, LIII (March 1, 1925), 661.

Innocence[6]

She tripped and fell against a star,
A lady we all have known;
Just what the villagers lusted for
To claim her one of their own;
Fallen but once the lower felt she,
So turned her face and died,—
With never a hounding fool to see
'Twas a star-lance in her side!

Neighbors[7]

Ah, you are cruel;
You ask too much;
Offered a hand, a finger-tip,
You must have a soul to clutch.

[Never underrate the courage]

Never underrate the courage
    nor weakness
    nor open power of a coward

his way is simply not one
of valiance but dalliance

Peeping from corners
crawling in your sleep
counting the moment
not the hour

6. First published in Cullen (ed.), *Caroling Dusk*, 51.
7. *Ibid.*, 47.

Sybil Speaks

"Young man, all you *touch* is what you lose
That you *keep* by *faith* you choose;
Lift your soul with wings on high,
Starve your body—even let it die!"

Questing[8]

Let me learn now where Beauty is;
My day is spent too far toward night
To wander aimlessly and miss her place;
To grope, eyes shut, and fingers touching space.

Her maidens I have known, seen durance beside,
Handmaidens to the Queen, whose duty bids
Them lie and lure afield their Vestal's acolyte,
Lest a human shake the throne, lest a god should know his might:
Nereid, daughter of the Trident, steering in her shell,
Paused in voyage, smile beguiling, tempted and I fell;
Spiteful dryads, sport forsaking, tossing birchen wreathes,
Left the Druidic priests they teased so
In the oaken trees, crying, "Ho a mortal! here a beliver!"
Bound me, she who held the sceptre, stricken by her, ah, deceiver . . .
But let me learn now where Beauty is;
I was born to know her mysteries,
And needing wisdom I must go in vain:
Being sworn bring to some hither land,
Leaf from her brow, light from her torchéd hand.

8. *Ibid.*, 48–49.

[God never planted a garden]

God never planted a garden
But He placed a keeper there;
And the keeper ever razed the ground
And built a city where
God cannot walk at the eve of day,
Nor take the morning air.

Change

This day is here I hoped would come at last,
When I, a man, should live again a tree
The dregs I drained with Life in days long passed
Now thru my body courage in ecstasy
Awhile I lived apprenticed warm to flesh
And son the passioned errands of the sun:
Where lifted on the wing of some bright mesh
Of streaming wind, or dropped too deep, and spun
Into some dark abyss of circling wave,—
If so a votary come to Charybdis
With his clear torch fed from a heart—and as brave
Still now that I am such a splendid tree
There is only God and man to buffet me.
Can only those who hate you, Life, know bliss . . .

[Thou art come to us, O God, this year]

Thou art come to us, O God, this year—
Or how come these wisteria boughs
Dripping with the heavy honey of the Spring
Art here. For who but Thou could in living bring
This loveliness beyond all
Our words for prayer
And blur of leafish shadows, leaf in ochre,
Orchid of bloom with bright tears
Of Thy April's grief
We thank Thee great God—

We who must now ever house
In the body-cramped places age has doomed—
That to us comes Even the sweet pangs
Of the Soul's illimitable sentience
Seeing the wisteria Thou has bloomed!

He Said:

"Your garden at dusk
Is the soul of love
Blurred in its beauty
And softly caressing;
I, gently daring
This sweetest confessing,
Say your garden at dusk
Is your soul, My Love."

Black Man O' Mine

Black man o' mine,
If the world were your lover,
It could not give what I give to you,
Or the ocean would yield and you could discover
Its ages of treasure to hold and to view;
Could it fill half the measure of my heart's portion . . .
Just for you living, just for you giving all this devotion,
Black man o' mine.

Black man o' mine,
As I hush and caress you, close to my heart,
All your loving is just your needing what's true;
Then with your passing dark comes my darkest part,
For living without your loving is only rue.
Black man o' mine, if the world were your lover
It could not give what I give to you.

For E. A. S.

This, then, entire, is what they say to me—
Demeanor peeved and fretted brow the while:
"So bad the man you sleep beside is free;
In lonely sadness must you go your mile:
He can not touch his lips to burning words
No image in his mind becomes his god;
He hears the sound of thrush and trilling birds—
Napt orchestra, like Caliban, to nod!"

The pity is that *they* should be such fools
As think weak traps may hold a fragrant breath;
That clumsy note played poorly still by rules
Can fill a life with living grace till death. . . .
Himself, the song my silly notes enjoy
His, too, the star I see, the dream employ.

Lines to a Nasturtium
(A Lover Muses)[9]

Flame-flower, Day-torch, Mauna Loa,
I saw a daring bee, today, pause, and soar,
   Into your flaming heart;
Then did I hear crisp, crinkled laughter
As the furies after tore him apart?
   A bird, next, small and humming,
Looked into your startled depths and fled. . . .
Surely, some dread sight, and dafter
   Than human eyes as mine can see,
Set the stricken air waves drumming
   In his flight.

Day-torch, Flame-flower, cool-hot Beauty,
I cannot see, I cannot hear your flutey
Voice lure your loving swain,
But I know one other to whom you are in beauty
Born in vain:

---

9. Slightly revised from the version as first published in *Palms*, IV (October, 1926), 13.

Hair like the setting sun,
Her eyes a rising star,
Motions gracious as reeds by Babylon, bar
All your competing;
Hands like, how like, brown lilies sweet,
Cloth of gold were fair enough to touch her feet . . .
Ah, how the sense reels at my repeating,
As once in her fire-lit heart I felt the furies
Beating, beating.

Life-Long, Poor Browning[10]

Life-long, poor Browning never knew Virginia,
Or he'd not grieved in Florence for April sallies
Back to English gardens after Euclid's linear:
Clipt yews, Pomander Walks, and pleachéd alleys;

Primroses, prim indeed, in quiet ordered hedges,
Waterways, soberly, sedately enchanneled,
No thin riotous blade even among the sedges,
All the wild country-side tamely impaneled . . .

Dead, now, dear Browning lives on in heaven,—
(Heaven's Virginia when the year's at its Spring)
He's haunting the byways of wine-aired leaven
And throating the notes of the wildings on wing:

Here canopied reaches of dogwood and hazel,
Beech tree and redbud fine-laced in vines,
Fleet clapping rills by lush fern and basil,
Drain blue hills to lowlands scented with pines . . .

Think you he meets in this tender green sweetness
Shade that was Elizabeth . . . immortal completeness!

10. First published in Cullen, *Caroling Dusk*, 49–50.

Any Wife to Any Husband:
A Derived Poem

This small garden is half my world
I am nothing to it—when all is said,
I plant the thorn and kiss the rose,
But they will grow when I am dead.

Let not this change, Love, the human life
Share with her the joy you had with me,
List with her the plaintive bird you heard with me.
Feel all human joys, but
Feel most a "shadowy third."

The Wife-Woman[11]

Maker-of-Sevens in the scheme of things
From earth to star;
Thy cycle holds whatever is fate, and
Over the border the bar.
Though rank and fierce the mariner
Sailing the seven seas,
He prays, as he holds his glass to his eyes,
Coaxing the Pleiades.

I cannot love them; and I feel your glad
Chiding from the grave,
That my all was only worth at all, what
Joy to you it gave,
These seven links the *Law* compelled
For the human chain—
I cannot love *them*; and *you*, oh,
Seven-fold months in Flanders slain!

A jungle there, a cave here, bred six
And a million years,
Sure and strong, mate for mate, such
Love as culture fears;

11. First published in Johnson (ed.), *The Book of American Negro Poetry*, 171–72.

I gave you clear the oil and wine;
You saved me your hob and hearth—
See how *even* life may be ere the
Sickle comes and leaves a swath.

But I can wait the seven of moons,
Or years I spare,
Hoarding the heart's plenty, nor spend
A drop, nor share—
So long but outlives a smile and
A silken gown;
Then gayly reach up from my shroud,
And you, glory-clad, reach down.

For Jim, Easter Eve[12]

If ever a garden was a Gethsemane,
with old tombs set high against
the crumpled olive tree—and lichen,
this, my garden has been to me.
For such as I none other is so sweet:
Lacking old tombs, here stands my grief,
and certainly its ancient tree.

Peace is here and in every season
a quiet beauty.
The sky falling about me
evenly to the compass . . .
What is sorrow but tenderness now
in this earth-close frame of land and sky
falling constantly into horizons
of east and west, north and south;
what is pain but happiness here
amid these green and wordless patterns,—
indefinite texture of blade and leaf:

Beauty of an old, old tree,
last comfort in Gethsemane.

---

12. Written in 1948 and first published in Langston Hughes and Arna Bontemps (eds.), *The Poetry of the Negro, 1746–1949* (Garden City, N. Y.: Doubleday, 1949), 65.

I Have a Friend[13]

I have a friend
And my heart from hence
Is closed to friendship,
Nor the gods' knees hold but one;
He watches with me thru the long night,
And when I call he comes,
Or when he calls I am there;
He does not ask me how beloved
Are my husband and children,
Nor ever do I require
Details of life and love
In the grave—his home,—
    We are such friends.

Translation[14]

We trekked into a far country,
My friend and I.
Our deeper content was never spoken,
But each knew all the other said.
He told me how calm his soul was laid
By the lack of anvil and strife.
"The wooing kestrel," I said, "mutes his mating-note
To please the harmony of this sweet silence."
And when at the day's end
We laid tired bodies 'gainst
The loose warm sands,
And the air fleeced its particles for a coverlet;
When star after star came out
To guard their lovers in oblivion—
My soul so leapt that my evening prayer
Stole my morning song!

13. First published in Cullen (ed.), *Caroling Dusk*, 47–48.
14. First published in Johnson (ed.), *The Book of American Negro Poetry*, 173.

[Dear Langston]

Dear Langston,

and *that* is what my days
have brought . . .
and this: lamp, odorless oil
round its long
dried wick:
Hope without wings
Love itself contemned
Where Michael broods,—
Arc after arc, you see,
If any where I own
A circle it is one
frustrate beginning—

Ascetic

Lord, still I am too strong—
   All Thy buffets fail,
But if I abstain . . . long,
   Will Thou make me frail?

When I love but lose,
   When I laugh . . . but cry
Full my deeper cruse,
   Will Thou tell me why . . . why!

Liability

Lord, Thy stripes for me,
For him the smoothéd pillow;
My eyes were clear
To see Thy golden stair,—
Be mine the willow.

Failure

Master, the harp is broken,
  Let me die;
Broken on a sobbing chord,
Riven by a single word,
Word by angels never spoken—
  Master, let me die.

Luther P. Jackson

There are men who died of grief
Because they could not wait.
Impatient were they of a hundred years, of a
Thousand, but a day.

  Die not of grief, men
We all must wait for sorrow,
Grief roughly breaks the Heart
But sorrow gently mends again.

Creed[15]

If my garden oak spares one bare ledge
For a boughed mistletoe to grow and wedge;
And all the wild birds this year should know
I cherish their freedom to come and go;
If a battered worthless dog, masterless, alone,
Slinks to my heels, sure of bed and bone;
And the boy just moved in, deigns a glance-assay,
Turns his pockets inside out, calls, "Come and play!"
If I should surprise in the eyes of my friend
That the deed was *my* favor he'd let me lend;
Or hear it repeated from a foe I despise,
That I whom he hated was chary of lies;
If a pilgrim stranger, fainting and poor,

15. First published in Cullen (ed.), *Caroling Dusk*, 51–52.

Followed an urge and rapped at my door,
And my husband loves me till death puts apart,
Less as flesh unto flesh, more as heart unto heart:
I may challenge God when we meet That Day,
And He dare not be silent or send me away.

The Sévignés

Down in Natchitoches there is a statue in a public square
A slave replica—not of Uncle Tom, praise God
But of Uncle Remus . . . a big plinth holding a little
              man bowing humbly to a master-mistress
This shameless thing set up to the intricate involvement
              of human slavery
Go, see it read it with whatever heart you have left.
No penance, callous beyond belief.
For these women who had so lately fled from the
              slavery of Europe to the great wilds of America.

White Things[16]

Most things are colorful things—the sky, earth, and sea.
              Black men are most men; but the white are free!
White things are rare things; so rare, so rare
They stole from out a silvered world—somewhere.
Finding earth-plains fair plains, save greenly grassed,
They strewed white feathers of cowardice, as they passed;
              The golden stars with lances fine
              The hills all red and darkened pine,
They blanched with their wand of power;
And turned the blood in a ruby rose
To a poor white poppy-flower.

16. First published in the *Crisis: A Record of the Darker Races*, XXV (March, 1923), 204.

They pyred a race of black, black men,
And burned them to ashes white; then,
Laughing, a young one claimed a skull,
For the skull of a black is white, not dull,
      But a glistening awful thing;
      Made, it seems, for this ghoul to swing
In the face of God with all his might,
And swear by the hell that siréd him:
      "Man-maker, make white!"

Grapes: Still-Life[17]

Snugly you rest, sweet globes,
Aged essence of the sun;
Copper of the platter
Like that you lie upon.

Is so well your heritage
You need feel no change
From the ringlet of your stem
To this bright rim's flange;

You green-white Niagara,
Cool dull Nordic of your kind,—
Does your thick meat flinch
From these . . . touch and press your rind?

Caco, there, so close to you,
Is the beauty of the vine;
Stamen red and pistil black
Thru the curving line;

Concord, the too peaceful one
Purpling at your side,
All the colors of his flask
Holding high in pride . . .

This, too, is your heritage,
You who force the plight;
Blood and bone you turn to them
For their root is white.

17. *Ibid.*, XXXVI (April, 1929), 124.

The Lemming: O Sweden

" . . . but," he said, "you just don't
understand politics, no woman
ever does. To the Eves of this world
every phase of it is a person game
played with the equation I-Me-Mine."

She: "For yourself, Sir, you are very old
academy. No new sense; those good clichés
when our earth was square, and
we all fell off the edge . . . or
could we turn back now to what
your apology asked when we
seemed to divide?"

He: "Yes, thank you—the scar?"

She: "They came on flowing, foodless—
mindless—plunging—war is so circle—
many butted into it where I stood on
the outside. One—it or epicene—
smaller, yet more lovely than the
rest, where winter had touched
the silver coat with sable—poor
creature, was errantly lamed . . .
my offense was pity, as I
leaned to help . . . it struck!"

[Untitled]

Terence MacSwiney
In days gone by many an Irish lad, had I called you
would have answered "I am here," for yours was only
a name to live by.
You raced with the wind along your glittering shore
Woke at dawn
Slept at eve
Ate what food
Drank what drink
Warmed by peat as you breathed it.

That was a boy's day
But one day you slept too long————
When you awoke you were a man—in a land you never saw before
Rightly nor had you known before the whole state
Stone on stone to house the rich,
Hovel on hovel to cover the poor
Talk is as the wind. What?
I have something—I can lay it down, I can take it up again
This I do for Erin, my beloved land.
Terence, Terence in glory forever,
Now lovers have another name to die by.

Letter to My Sister[18]

It is dangerous for a woman to defy the gods;
To taunt them with the tongue's thin tip,
Or strut in the weakness of mere humanity,
Or draw a line daring them to cross;
The gods own the searing lightning,
The drowning waters, tormenting fears
And anger of red sins.

Oh, but worse still if you mince timidly—
Dodge this way or that, or kneel or pray,
Be kind, or sweat agony drops
Or lay your quick body over your feeble young;
If you have beauty or none, if celibate
Or vowed—the gods are Juggernaut,
Passing over . . . over . . .

This you may do:
Lock your heart, then, quietly,
And lest they peer within,
Light no lamp when dark comes down
Raise no shade for sun;
Breathless must your breath come through
If you'd die and dare deny
The gods their god-like fun.

18. Revised from the version originally titled "Sybil Warns Her Sister" and first published in Charles S. Johnson (ed.), *Ebony and Topaz: A Collectanea* (New York: National Urban League, 1927), 94.

Before the Feast at Shushan[19]

Garden of Shushan!
After Eden, all terrace, pool, and flower recollect thee:
Ye weavers in saffron and haze and Tyrian purple,
Tell yet what range in color wakes the eye;
Sorcerer, release the dreams born here when
Drowsy, shifting palm-shade enspells the brain;
And sound! ye with harp and flute ne'er essay
Before these star-noted birds escaped from paradise awhile to
Stir all dark, and dear, and passionate desire, till mine
Arms go out to be mocked by the softly kissing body of the wind—
Slave, send Vashti to her King!

The fiery wattles of the sun startle into flame
The marbled towers of Shushan:
So at each day's wane, two peers—the one in
Heaven, the other on earth—welcome with their
Splendor the peerless beauty of the Queen.

Cushioned at the Queen's feet and upon her knee
Finding glory for mine head,—still, nearly shamed
Am I, the King, to bend and kiss with sharp
Breath the olive-pink of sandaled toes between;
Or lift me high to the magnet of a gaze, dusky,
Like the pool when but the moon-ray strikes to its depth;
Or closer press to crush a grape 'gainst lips redder
Than the grape, a rose in the night of her hair;
Then—Sharon's Rose in my arms.

And I am hard to force the petals wide;
And you are fast to suffer and be sad.
Is any prophet come to teach a new thing
Now in a more apt time?
Have him 'maze how you say love is sacrament;
How says Vashti, love is both bread and wine;
How to the altar may not come to break and drink,
Hulky flesh nor fleshly spirit!

19. First published in the *Crisis*, XIX (February, 1920), 186.

I, thy lord, like not manna for meat as a Judahn;
I, thy master, drink, and red wine, plenty, and when
I thirst. Eat meat, and full, when I hunger.
I, thy King, teach you and leave you, when I list.
No woman in all Persia sets out strange action
To confuse Persia's lord—
Love is but desire and thy purpose fulfillment;
I, thy King, so say!

Po' Little Lib

Half-inch brown spider,
    black-spotted back
Moves thru the grass,
    white-sheeted pack.
M-O-V-E-S thru the grass, O god
if it chance
For the drought driven air turns leaf into lance

Run, escape, wee one you are free . . .
How delicately she re-knits her vast pain
Chance did set her free
What bound her again?

Epitome

Once the world was young
For I was twenty and very old
And you and I knew all the answers
What the day was, how the hours would turn
One dial was there to see
Now the world is old and I am still young
For the young know nothing, nothing.

Dunbar[20]

Ah, how poets sing and die!
Make one song and Heaven takes it;
Have one heart and Beauty breaks it;
Chatterton, Shelley, Keats and I—
Ah, how poets sing and die!

[Earth, I thank you]

Earth, I thank you
for the pleasure of your language
You've had a hard time
bringing it to me
from the ground
to grunt thru the noun
To all the way
feeling   seeing   smelling   touching
—awareness
I am here!

Requiem[21]

Oh, I who so wanted to own some earth,
Am consumed by the earth instead:
Blood into river
Bone into land
   The grave restores what finds its bed.

Oh, I who did drink of Spring's fragrant clay,
Give back its wine for other men:
Breath into air
Heart into grass
   My heart bereft—I might rest then.

20. First published *ibid.*, XXI (November, 1920), 32.
21. First published in the *Lyric* (Spring, 1931), 3.

Selected Bibliography

Addington, Richard, ed. *Letters of Madame de Sévigné to Her Daughter and Her Friends*. London: Routledge and Kegan Paul, 1937.

Altman, Bruno. "Afrika in Amerika." *Die Woche*, January 12, 1929, pp. 49–51.

Brown, Sterling Allen. *Negro Poetry and Drama*. Washington, D.C.: Associates in Negro Folk Education, 1937.

————. *Southern Road*. New York: Harcourt, Brace and Co., 1932.

Bryce, James. *The American Commonwealth*. New York: Macmillan and Co., 1888.

Buchanan-Gould, Vera. *Not Without Laughter: The Life and Writings of Olive Schreiner*. London: Hutchinson and Co., 1949.

Casey, Alfredo, trans. and ed. *Dos Siglos De Poesia Norteamericana Poetas Blancos Y Negros De Los EE. UU*. Buenos Aires, Argentina: Editorial Claridad, 1947. This book contains a critical note on Anne Spencer and Spanish translations of "Dunbar" and "I Have a Friend."

Cullen, Countee, ed. *Caroling Dusk: An Anthology of Verse by Negro Poets*. New York: Harper & Brothers, 1927.

Davis, Arthur P., and Saunders Redding, eds. *Cavalcade: Negro American Writing from 1760 to the Present*. Boston: Houghton Mifflin Co., 1971.

Ellmann, Richard, and Robert O'Clair, eds. *The Norton Anthology of Modern Poetry*. New York: W. W. Norton & Co., 1973.

Hammersley, Violet, trans. and ed. *Letters from Madame La Marquise de Sévigné*. London: Secker and Warburg, 1955.

Huggins, Nathan Irvin. *Harlem Renaissance*. New York: Oxford University Press, 1971.

Hughes, Langston. "The Negro Artist and the Racial Mountain." *Nation*, June 23, 1926, pp. 692–94.

Hughes, Langston, and Arna Bontemps, eds. *The Poetry of the Negro, 1746–1949*. Garden City, N.Y.: Doubleday and Co., 1949.

James Weldon Johnson Memorial Collection of Negro Arts and Letters. Collection of American Literature, Beinecke Rare Book and Manuscript Library, Yale University.

Johnson, Charles Spurgeon, ed. *Ebony and Topaz: A Collectanea*. New York: National Urban League, 1927.

Johnson, James Weldon. *Along This Way: The Autobiography of James Weldon Johnson*. New York: Viking Press, 1933.

——, ed. *The Book of American Negro Poetry*. New York: Harcourt, Brace and Co., 1922.

Kerlin, Robert T., ed. *Negro Poets and Their Poems*. Washington, D.C.: Associated Publishers, 1923.

Maugham, William Somerset. "Preface" to *Letters from Madame La Marquise de Sévigné*. Translated and edited by Violet Hammersley. London: Secker and Warburg, 1955.

O'Hagarty, P. S. *A Short Memoir of Terence MacSwiney*. Dublin: Talbot Press, 1922.

Rosenberger, Francis Coleman. *Virginia Reader: A Treasury of Writings from the First Voyages to the Present*. New York: E. P. Dutton, 1948.

Shepperson, George, and Thomas Price. *Independent African: John Chilembwe and the Origins, Settings and Significance of the Nyasaland Native Rising of 1915*. Edinburg, Scotland: University of Edinburg Press, 1958. Having been Chilembwe's schoolmate at Virginia Seminary, Mrs. Spencer provided the authors with personal recollections of him. The authors can attribute Chilembwe's unusual academic knowledge in certain areas only to the high level of instruction going on at the seminary in the late nineteenth century. See Chapter 2 herein. See also Shepperson's chapter on Lynchburg.

Spencer, Chauncey E. Papers. Bentley Historical Library, University of Michigan, Ann Arbor.

Spencer Family Papers. Anne Spencer House and Garden Historic Landmark. Lynchburg, Virginia.

Thirty Years of Lynching in the United States, 1889–1919. New York: NAACP, 1919.

Thomas, Jerry Bruce. "Coal Country: The Rise of the Southern Smokeless Coal Industry and Its Effect on Area Development, 1872–1910." Ph.D. dissertation, University of North Carolina at Chapel Hill, 1971.

de Tocqueville, Alexis Charles Henri Maurice Clerel. *Democracy in America*. Translated by Henry Reve, revised and edited by Francis Bowen. 3rd ed. Cambridge: Sever and Francis, 1863.

Untermeyer, Louis. *American Poetry Since 1900*. New York: H. Holt and Co., 1923.

Wagner, Jean. *Black Poets of the United States from Paul Laurence Dunbar to Langston Hughes*. Translated by Kenneth Douglas. Urbana: University of Illinois Press, 1973.

Index